a six-wee

MW00622439

in the wait

Heidi Anderson • Courtney Frasier
Holly Holt • Amanda Jass • Chelsea Ritchie

table of contents

a note from the authors

Dear Friend,

We are so happy to be spending the next six weeks with you! If you are holding this book, chances are you are all too familiar with the word *wait*. Perhaps you're waiting for an exciting thing ahead or maybe you're waiting for healing, whether physical, emotional, or spiritual. So much of life is made up of seasons of waiting—however, waiting doesn't have to be a negative thing!

Our lives often weave seamlessly in and out of these seasons. Breakthroughs, families, jobs, graduations, homes, and health may all be things you are desperately waiting for. Waits can be exciting, a little scary, moderately annoying, or painfully unbearable. We can all probably relate to a wait, whether now or in the past, that has been all-consuming, that takes our thoughts hostage and doesn't allow us to think of anything else. Our prayer for this devotional is that we would be reminded of this important truth: God can use seasons of waiting for our growth and His glory.

It might be hard to believe that there is a purpose to some of the most uncertain, frustrating, and seemingly stagnant times in our lives. But there is! However, we won't likely uncover what those reasons are if we simply sit back and check out. We need to be present through it all in order to understand what God wants to do in and through us during our waiting seasons. That's what this study is all about!

God knows right where you are at this moment, and He has a plan for you. God also recognizes that waiting is a normal part of our lives. Romans 8:25 reads, "But if we hope for what we do not see, we wait for it with patience."

Learning how to embrace the wait may not be easy, but through it, we believe God has so much for us to learn. We are excited for you to learn His truths with us over the next several weeks!

Much love,
Heidi, Courtney, Holly, Amanda, and Chelsea

P.S. Find us on Instagram at @inthewaitstudy and use #InTheWaitStudy on social media to connect with others (and us!) on what you are learning throughout the devotional. Let's fill our feeds with encouragement and lessons learned "in the wait"!

how to use this study

In your hands is an interactive devotional. Throughout this study, you will be asked to read, think, dive deeper, and reflect. Here's what we think you might need in order to make the most of this study:

- <u>Your Bible</u>. If you don't have one, don't worry! Websites such as bible.com and apps such as YouVersion keep Scripture right at our fingertips. These resources are free and will allow you to look up passages and compare translations. Unless otherwise noted, all verses are quoted in this study are from the *English Standard Version®* (ESV®).

- <u>Your pen.</u> Throughout the days, you will see blank spaces for you to answer questions, write out Scripture, journal your thoughts, and reflect on the lessons you're learning. Feel free to use the blank space as your heart needs. And doodlers: doodle on!

We want this study to be something you can use during your devotional time or thrown in a purse to be read on the go. Remember, it's not about having the perfect quiet time or prayer ritual, but rather choosing to build a relationship and spend time with our Creator. Here's what you can expect in the following pages.

weekly content breakdown

<u>Day One: Introduction</u>. The first day of each week will give you a new author's perspective and an overview of what topic will be covered that week. Use this day to ask God what He wants you to learn throughout the week. You'll see space to jot down your thoughts and prayers.

<u>Days Two-Six: Lessons</u>. Here is where the week's author will jump into the content. You will see opportunities throughout each lesson to respond. We hope you don't skip over these! Each lesson will end with a *Dive Deeper* section, which gives you the opportunity to read more in His Word, a *Reflection* section, which allows you to critically think about what you've learned and how you will apply it, and a prayer.

<u>Day Seven: Conclusion</u>. This last day will give you a chance to wrap up the week and reflect on what you have learned. Again, use the space to process the lessons God has spoken to you so you can look back on them in the future.

So let's dive in! We have poured our hearts into this study, knowing God has placed it into your hands with a purpose. We pray each section blesses you and your heart is open to the lessons waiting seasons can teach us.

listening in the wait

Life doesn't begin when a waiting season is over. Life is happening *right now*. Are we living? Living to the fullest?

In John 10, Jesus says we absolutely can live every season in our lives to its fullest potential. It's what He intends for us.

We don't have to do it all on our own—there's hope because Jesus is our Ultimate Guide. Through the ups and the downs, we can learn to listen to Jesus' voice in our hearts. He's there, waiting to have a two-way conversation, waiting to lead us into refinement, into His plans, into a deeper relationship with Himself.

As I wait for the next chapter in my life to unfold, I don't want to regret this season by walking through it half-heartedly. If this is the season God wants me in, how will I listen to Him as He lets me know what this season is about? We do not have to walk through life blindly. God has a purpose for this season of waiting.

It's easy to wish away the waiting. Let's not minimize a season God is asking us to maximize. Let's press into Him, and press into all that He has to say to us *right now.*

prepare your heart for the week

This week, we get to think about and learn about what *listening in the wait* looks like in our lives. How are you listening for God's voice? What do you want to learn this week about listening for God's guidance in your current season? Think about these questions. Ask God what He wants you to take away from this week's topic.

overcoming lies

*Listen to my voice in the morning, Lord. Each morning I
bring my requests to you and wait expectantly.*
PSALM 5:3

Sometimes lies are stored up in our hearts without us
even knowing it. A few years ago, I came face to face with
an icky lie.

I didn't believe God would actually show up when I
waited expectantly for Him in prayer. Reasons swirled
around my head: *You're not good enough. You haven't told
enough people about Jesus. You blew it. God doesn't want to
waste His time on you.* These lies kept me from waiting in
expectation for God to whisper into my life.

Waiting in expectation for God to be God is so
comforting when we believe He will actually reveal Himself

to us. But what if that's hard to believe? When the voice in the back of our heads says, *Don't ask because He won't respond,* we end up in waiting seasons discouraged, hopeless, and trying to take control.

Some of us believe God speaks to others, but He doesn't speak to us. We believe He can, but He chooses not to because of who we are and what we've done. Take a moment to reflect: Do you believe God can and will reply to your prayers when you wait expectantly for Him?

Yes, as I see it happened.

It is all too easy to believe God doesn't want to speak into our lives. It's safer that way, isn't it? At least it *feels* safer.

Have you ever told a story, and no one else laughed? Have you ever shared a part of your heart with a friend, and they stared back at you with a blank face? Or worse, minimized your feelings?

Waiting in expectation for God to reply to our thoughts feels scary for some of us because we fear rejection. Who wants to pour their heart out to God, ask Him for guidance, and then hear nothing but crickets? Not me!

But good news: Jesus says those who come to Him, He will never reject (John 6:37). We are fully accepted by God—both in our prayers and in our waiting.

There are so many things we humans wait for. Daily things like the stoplight to turn green, the hot tea to cool, the paint to dry. More complex waiting seasons weave throughout our lives as well like waiting for a job, financial stability, a spouse, a pregnancy, dreams to be realized. Reality is, these things may or may not come. The only certain thing we can wait for and expect is this: for God to lead and to guide us.

We know God speaks to and guides His children in different ways. We see examples of God's creative communication style all throughout the Bible: Moses—a burning bush. Balaam—a talking donkey. Saul—a vision. David—his friend Nathan. God reveals Himself to each of us in the most unique ways. For you, it may be a song. A friend's word. An image. His Word.

But so often, it's hard to hear God speaking to us above the lies and above the noise of this modern day world.

There have been times in my life where I pray, and I get nothing. No pointing finger from the sky. No booming voice speaking from the heavens. In many waiting seasons, there are decisions we are faced with. And we need direction. *Now.* But we get no answer!

And like a little girl whose dad ignores her yet again, we slump off believing God doesn't care about us and He doesn't want to direct us. The lies can echo in our hearts: *Rejected. Unimportant. Alone.*

Ah! We cannot let these lies stick in our minds and in our hearts! We are accepted! Important! Not abandoned! Friend, *keep pressing into what God has to say!*

Psalm 95:7 (TLB) says, "Oh, that you would hear him calling you today and come to him!" What sticks out to you about this verse?

The truth is no matter what kind of season we're in—a season of waiting for a joyous event or just to make it out of a season of grief—God walks with us and He is near.

As we call out to God, *God calls our names in return.* What an astonishing thought!

Imagine something for a moment. You say, "Dear God..." and before you can get out another word, He interrupts you right then and there...

And calls your name in return.

"Hi Sarah." "Hey Kim." "Hello Molly."

In the Old Testament, in 1 Samuel 3, Samuel is sleeping when he hears his name called. He runs to Eli, the priest he was with. Eli, confused, declared, "I didn't call you, my son [...] Go back to bed" (NIV, v. 6). This happened three times, and "[t]hen Eli realized it was the Lord who was calling the boy" (v. 8).

What a visual! In verse 7 it says, "Samuel did not yet know the Lord because he had never had a message from the Lord before." However, as soon as Samuel knew the Lord and understood what the Lord's voice sounded like, he was able to recognize it!

Eli knew the Lord, and he was able to recognize the Lord's voice in Samuel's life. As we learn what the Lord's voice sounds like in our lives, how important it is for us to have Elis in our lives, too. When we surround ourselves with people who have shown they recognize the Lord's still small voice, they may be able to point out that God is speaking to us, but maybe we just haven't learned what His voice sounds like in our lives.

As we continue to cultivate our relationship with the Lord like Eli, we may, for the first time, begin to recognize how the Lord is calling out to us like Samuel. As you continue to seek God in this season of waiting, you can overcome the lies swirling in your head, and you can start to believe as you call out to God, He is calling out to you in return—let's wait expectantly for Him!

12-27-18

What kind of season of waiting are you in right now?

Waiting for gods gift (baby)

Are there any lies in your heart that stop you from believing
Jesus is speaking to you in this season? Write out these
untruths. If you are feeling bold, say these lies out loud. Then,
declare that they are not true, and speak the opposite into
your life.

That I need to work hard & struggle
That I am not capable

How do these words of Jesus apply to you?

"I am with you always, even to the end of the age."
Matthew 28:20b (NKJV)

That for every season, circumstances,
in any
or ~~even~~ given situation god is with

me.

"...The sheep recognize [the Shepherd's] voice and come
to him. He calls his own sheep by name and leads them
out. After he has gathered his own flock, he walks ahead
of them, and they follow him because they know his
voice." John 10:3b-4

reflection

Take some time to ask God how He speaks to you
personally. If you don't believe He does, tell Him why you
believe that.

*Dear God, I want to believe You can and will speak to me,
that You can guide me, that You want to guide me. But
sometimes I doubt that You are active in this season. I want
to pray in faith and in expectation. I pray You would help me
hear Your voice calling out to me in return. Amen.*

Talking

Father, if you will, please don't make me suffer
by having me drink from this cup.
LUKE 22:42 (CEV)

I sat down with my friend in a coffee shop. The espresso machine hummed. The blenders made a racket. The metal ice scooper wrangled in the remaining cubes. We chit-chatted and then, the real talk came.

"I'm confused and I don't know what's going on." In the midst of this noisy, public place, I shared the real stuff. The vulnerable stuff. The honest stuff. All the while, a suave man browsed Facebook on his phone next to us.

As I got in the car, a thought popped into my head. *Am I ever that real with God?* I scrunched my face, instantly uncomfortable. I left that question unanswered.

Waiting seasons can be exciting. We wait for the wedding day to approach. The promotion right around the corner. The baby to be born. Other times, waiting is confusing and painful. We don't know if there will be a "when." We don't even know if there will be an "if." When the season continues longer than we think it should, we begin to question if God is even on our side. When we give in to these thoughts, praying honest prayers feels unsafe. So we guard our hearts before the Lord—oftentimes without knowing it.

Even after I got out of that car, the unanswered question followed me around. I couldn't shake it. We are so willing to talk about our confusion, frustrations, and longings to friends or on social media, so what keeps us from that same kind of real talk with God?

Jesus shows us something about real talk. It's a powerful example. Throughout the Gospels, Jesus was in a waiting season. A waiting season for his death. Intense? Yes.

Look up Luke 22:39-44 in the CEV version if possible—what does this passage say?

When I read this, I imagine Jesus prayed out loud to the Father. He gets honest. He says, "Father, if you will, please

don't make me suffer by having me drink from this cup..."
(v. 42).

Read that again and let it sit with you for a moment.

Jesus—the Son of God—got real. He asked and confessed something that is mind blowing. It's out in the open, to God, and with His disciples just a stone's throw away.

Jesus asked the Father, if He willed, to take all of it away: the arrest, the beatings, the crucifixion. He knew what was coming. He knew all of it.

As the Father heard Jesus ask for the rescue-of-the-world-plan to be taken away, God doesn't say, "Oh, Jesus. You know what—that was an unacceptable emotion to have." He doesn't say, "Why would You even ask that? That's dumb." He doesn't say, "I'm really disappointed You just told me that. This Savior-of-the-world thing has been thousands of years in the making. You want to quit now? Should I call You a quitter?"

God's actual reaction was this: He heard Jesus' honest prayer and then, "An angel from heaven appeared to Him and strengthened Him" (v. 43). Jesus was in so much anguish! But His confession to God opened up an opportunity for God to send help. Jesus WAS strengthened and because of it, He prayed even more earnestly than before.

This passage helped answer my unanswered question: The reason I don't get real with God is honesty. I realized I talk with my friends more openly and honestly than I prayed to God.

God got my thoughts masked in a proper, ritualized prayer voice. My friends got my laughter, my joyous reactions, my tears, and my honest confusion. What if I talked out loud to God like I do to my friends?

Have you ever straight up talked out loud to God? Not prayed. Talked. Like, laid it *all* out there? Maybe screamed, shouted, yelled? We know that God can handle our fear. God can hear our doubting. God understands when there is something we dread and we simply don't have the strength to do it. In our waiting seasons, our thoughts don't shake God. They can shake us. But they don't shake God.

Talking out loud to an invisible God maybe sounds weird, and maybe it is. It's certainly vulnerable and makes me uncomfortable to hear the actual thoughts of my heart spoken out loud. But maybe, just maybe, we can learn something from Jesus about prayer. He took His deepest desires and requests and got them out into the light of day. He trusted God to do what God wanted to do, but it didn't stop Him from being honest. After He makes known His heart, He says, "[D]o what you want, and not what I want" (v. 42). What a beautiful example of a prayer Jesus has given us.

I invite you to talk out loud to God. Give it a try. Get honest before Him, and listen for His whisper. Let's wait in expectation for God's strength to arrive in whatever circumstance we are in.

dive deeper

Read Luke 22:39-44 out loud. What challenges you about this passage? What phrases stick out to you?

Father if you are willing, take this cup from me; yet not my will, but yours be done

What is an area of your life right now that you need extra strength in? Look up Psalm 121. Which phrases encourage you most?

The Lord will keep you from all harm he will watch over your life

David's prayers are honest prayers. What is David being honest about in these Psalms? Which can you relate to the most?

Psalm 3:1-2

Psalm 5:1

Psalm 13

Psalm 139

Why are honest prayers important while listening for God's whisper in the wait?

So that god knows whats in our heart.

reflection

What is something you doubt in your season of waiting?
Talk to God about it, and know your doubts, questions, and
confessions don't shake God. Listen for His truth, and let it
strengthen you as you call out to Him.

*Lord, help me be more honest in my prayers so You can
continue to reveal Your power to me. I want to be more
vulnerable with You! Please provide me courage to share my
real thoughts with You. Amen.*

listening

But Jonah got up and went in the opposite direction
to get away from the Lord.
JONAH 1:2a

I saw her mouth moving, but I couldn't understand a single word she said. I was in Italy. On a noisy, cramped, and smelly bus.

Her accent was different than my ears were used to. Even though she was fluent in English, I needed to give all my attention to her unfamiliar voice.

Conversations were happening all around me. Italian horns sounded outside the bus windows. Gelato dripped down the arm of the kid in front of me. There were so many distractions. I couldn't focus. I couldn't understand her. I couldn't respond.

This scene reminds me a little bit of trying to find some quiet minutes to spend with God. During our busy schedules, we try intently to listen to His still small voice. But the environments we are in and the distractions we face make it nearly impossible to stop and listen!

When we think about how we try to listen to God in the waiting season, where are we located? A noisy Italian bus? All too often, our commitments scream at us from all directions. We wonder why we are depleted. Why our hope wavers. Why we want to toss in the towel.

Everyone's heart-ears engage in different ways. Scripture often describes Jesus as withdrawing from the crowds and the chaos, to go to a quiet place to pray. Maybe your "quiet place" is in nature. Maybe it's playing a guitar. Maybe it's cooking. We all connect with God in different ways, and thus, He connects with us all in individual ways.

Whatever your quiet place is, God uses these still moments to bring a thought to our minds. Encouragement to our hearts. Reassurance to our plans. Actions steps to take.

During our waiting seasons, do we do this enough? Do we complain about not knowing what to do yet fail to seek God?

Spending time with God isn't for religious points. It isn't a "have" to. It's not an obligation. God doesn't base His love for us on how many devotions we do! But, in order to get through this crazy thing called life, God knows being connected to Him is our only means of soul-survival and sanity. He continually beckons us to Himself. It's why we were created.

If I am honest, there are times I do NOT want to spend time with God. Nope. I feel too hurt. You didn't answer my prayer. That bad thing happened.

In these times, why is it so easy to run away? God is and always will be faithful. So what happens? Sometimes we don't want to hear a "no" or a "yes" or a "go". So we just stop spending time with Him. We stop listening. We stop waiting in expectation.

Can you relate? Let's think about a specific reason or area we may be avoiding God. Now read Jonah 1:1-6. Ask God if there is anything you can learn from Jonah in this passage. Write out some thoughts.

Listen to word of god.
Obedience.

I have to laugh—Jonah actually thought he was going to escape from the Lord. But running from the Lord was nearly the death of him! If we read on, Jonah is thrown overboard to quiet the storm and a large fish swallows him up to keep him from drowning. *Sheesh.* Talk about a story.

Is it any different for us? Waiting seasons ask us to have patience. On top of that, God then asks us to trust Him in seemingly illogical circumstances. And then He asks us to obey.

Sometimes, we don't like to obey. We don't like it one bit! We run back onto the Italian bus (or hop a ship to Tarshish) in hopes to drown out the small voice of God in our spirits.

Every time I've done this, it hasn't ended well. I regret the time I've spent distracted, I regret not trusting in my God, and I learn that I am more like Jonah that I would like to admit.

Life and waiting seasons are so much better connected to God. We weren't made to journey without Him. His whisper leads us to the right path, and He strengthens us for another day.

At times, we aren't ready to obey, so we stay on the dock. We aren't fleeing to Tarshish but we also aren't boarding the boat to Nineveh.

Why don't we *tell* God that we aren't ready to obey instead of fleeing?

I've had times where I've said, "God, I don't want to spend time with you. I feel hurt." Or, "I'm scared of what You're going to say or ask me to do."

It may feel strange or perhaps disrespectful to tell God we don't like what He said or that we don't want to obey His direction, but guess what? *God can handle our feelings.* When we shoot straight with God, we are able to be honest with ourselves. Honesty with God keeps the path of communication open. God uses that to meet us where we are emotionally and spiritually. He will help us make the right steps toward obedience in our waiting seasons. It may not be easy, but He is the master of encouragement.

In every day and in every season, our relationship with the Lord will look different. Some days we'll crave to spend time with God, and other days we may not think about Him for a moment. Some days we run in the opposite direction, and other days we wholeheartedly dive into the next step God has. Let's not compare this season with last season or with your friend's season. God is teaching us how to live fully right now. We may be on our way to Tarshish. We may be on our way to Nineveh. We may still be on the dock. But let's get to our "quiet place"; let's talk to God honestly, and let's wait in expectation for Him to give us the strength to obey His guidance.

dive deeper

Where is a place you feel very connected to God? How can you make it a priority in your daily or yearly schedule?

In our room. Night time.

Is there an area in your life where God is asking you to obey Him? Talk with God about what may be stopping you or what you may be afraid of. Read Jonah 1:1-6 again.

Yes, comparing this to the last season.

Think about your waiting season and a decision you may be facing. Are you on your way to Tarshish, Nineveh, or are you still on the dock? Write out some reasons you are where you are.

reflection

Sometimes past hurts or a poor church experience makes us run away from God. Think about any areas where you may need your heart to be mended. Reflect upon Psalm 147:3 "He heals the brokenhearted and binds up their wounds." Ask God to show you areas of brokenheartedness and ask Him to start to heal your heart so you can step into obedience.

Dear God, in this season, empower me and give me discipline to spend time with You. I ask You would help me love You and the people around me better. Give me courage to obey You when You ask me to do something difficult. Amen.

accepted

I am the Lord God. I am merciful and very patient with my
people. I show great love, and I can be trusted.
EXODUS 34:6 (CEV)

My sister is four years older than me. When she officially
became a teenager, she had shampoo that only she could
use. Why? Because it was called TeenSpirit and in her
words, "You can't use it, Courtney. You're not a teenager
yet."

The black bottle stared at me from the corner of our
yellow-tiled bathtub. The design, the shape, the words
TeenSpirit emblazoned on the front... it was all so... cool. I
wanted to be a teen. That shampoo was one step closer.

One night, after many nights of holding off, I just
couldn't resist the temptation anymore! I remember using the

forbidden shampoo. As I was lathering up my long hair, guilt washed over me like the water.

As soon as I left the bathroom, I saw her. I couldn't bear to look at her! I felt like my head turned *into* the bottle of shampoo. Seeing through my acting-weirdly-because-I'm-obviously-guilty behavior, she approached me, "Did you use my shampoo?" Older sisters know everything, I swear.

In my nine-year-old head, there was no greater embarrassment than getting caught. So I lied straight through my teeth. "No." But older sisters always have a one-up on the younger.

She walked straight into the bathroom, sniffed the air, and knowingly said, "Then why does it smell like Bahama Breeze in here?" I'm sure I turned 18 shades of red. (My fair skin can't hide embarrassment.) She reiterated what I already knew very well, "You can't use it, Courtney. You're not a teenager yet." Oh, the woes of a nine-year-old.

Sometimes we're caught trying to make our seasons of waiting go a little quicker. Even when we know it isn't the right thing for us, taking control is sometimes easier than trusting God.

We date the guy who isn't right. We make friends with the wrong kind of crowd. We take a job that compromises our values. We spend our time on wrong things to make the pain go away.

Then our lives begin to smell like the thing we shouldn't have done. We hope God doesn't sniff us out! But when He does, what will His reaction be?

Is this image of God as familiar to you as it was for me? You come to God and ask for help or for forgiveness. God, with crossed arms, a disappointed look on His face, and with impatience shakes His head and says, "Again?"

Think for a moment: when you come to God, what's your picture of God? What is His body language, His facial expressions, and His tone of voice? Write it out.

Exodus 34:6 in the CEV tells us the truth about God. It says, "I am the Lord God. I am merciful and very patient with my people. I show great love, and I can be trusted."

Does what you wrote down match the description of God in this verse?

So often, we have the wrong picture of God. Perhaps your view of God is one of anger, disappointment, or disgust. Look up Romans 8:1 and write it out.

You may have heard this verse before. But let's be reminded together of a great truth. We know God doesn't speak to His children in harsh tones. Why? All God's wrath landed on Jesus on the cross. As Christians, God's wrath doesn't land on us again! There is no condemnation. Our sin is already paid for.

Yes, we will mess up. We will make mistakes. We will try and run ahead of Him. I'm pretty sure I've sprinted whole marathons and made it to the finish line before I realized what I had done!

But Jesus is always there for us—and His voice, tone, and body language will never condemn us, never belittle us. When we come to Jesus, He will be waiting for us to talk with Him about what our hearts have inside of them. He will be patient, slow to anger, and abounding in steadfast love.

Hebrews 4:15 in the NIV says, "For we do not have a high priest who is unable to empathize with our weaknesses, but we have one who has been tempted in every way, just as we are— yet he did not sin."

This is a powerful truth. Jesus empathizes with our weaknesses. When we take control to try to speed up waiting, guess what? He gets it. *I know you want a spouse. I know you want a friend. I know you want security. I know you want to feel normal again. I understand. I know all of this is so hard.*

Whoa. Jesus gets what we are going through because He experienced temptations, too. He empathizes and then asks us to continue to trust and obey Him in our seasons.

As we think about the seasons we are in today, let's come before God with a fresh perspective. As we listen to Him and for Him in the waiting, let's allow God to help us believe that His tone is merciful, patient, and loving. He doesn't shame us. His timing can be trusted. Let's approach Him believing we can receive His gentle whisper. Even if we feel like our heads have turned into giant shampoo bottles, He doesn't turn us away.

dive deeper

Look up Isaiah 40:11 and 1 John 4:16. What do these verses teach us about the character and nature of God?

- god takes care of his people. He holds them close.

- god lives in them.

Read 1 Corinthians 13. As you read this passage, replace the word 'love' with 'God'. What is something new you have learned about God through this passage?

That god is love ☺

reflection

Talk with God about your view of Him. Ask Him how your view of Him got to be that way. If you need to, ask God to heal any areas of your heart that view Him as harsh, passive, angry, etc.

Dear God, thank you that You are patient with Your children. Please help me understand more fully what it means that You are <u>merciful</u>, <u>patient</u>, <u>loving</u>, and <u>trustworthy</u>. In this season of waiting, help me learn more about those qualities as I seek to continue to know You more. Amen.

silent snow

As the rain and the snow come down from heaven, and do not return to it without watering the earth and making it bud and flourish, so that it yields seed for the sower and bread for the eater, so is my word that goes out from my mouth: It will not return to me empty, but will accomplish what I desire and achieve the purpose for which I sent it. You will go out in joy and be led forth in peace; the mountains and hills will burst into song before you, and all the trees of the field will clap their hands. Instead of the thornbush will grow the juniper, and instead of briers the myrtle will grow. This will be for the Lord's renown, for an everlasting sign, that will endure forever.

ISAIAH 55:10-13

Last spring, I heard something strange on the radio. "Minnesota is in a moderate drought." What? Drought? After winter? I never heard of such a thing before! To me, drought was 100 degree temps and sunshine for weeks. But as I listened to the radio, it began to make sense. Our snowfall was less than normal this winter. What I had never realized before was that snow actually waters the earth in springtime! Without enough snow during winter, the flourishing that should happen during springtime suffers.

As we listen during our wait, God compares His words not only to rain, but also to snow. So what's the difference?

In some seasons, He speaks to us abundantly. His words are like rain, and our souls are instantly watered. We bud and we flourish. God is good.

Then winter hits unexpectedly. From summer to winter—from rain to snow—from hearing God's voice to silence. Did I do something wrong?

I have experienced this many times in my life. Have you experienced this as well? Not until recently have I been able to understand it just a little bit more.

In seasons of what feels like silence, God's words may be like gentle snow falling in our lives without a sound. The snow is accumulating in our souls without realization. In our limited perspective, we feel cold and God's silence feels colder.

This gentle, silent, snowfall is just like the rain, and is accomplishing something in our lives. God sends His words in snowflakes when He knows instant watering would not yield the type of fruit He wants for us. He may be building endurance. Maybe trust. Maybe joy. Maybe perseverance.

And then, when the time is right, God will begin to send sunshine to melt the snow. Like a cool glass of water for a parched tongue, the snow starts to melt, gradually, watering, watering, watering. Our souls have endured a winter. God has been with us all along. The budding and flourishing of springtime is a result of the silent snow melting. How joyous it is!

Why does this happen? Isaiah says, the snow and the rain, the watering and the growing, is all to make God known in our lives and for us to give Him the glory.

After seasons of rain and seasons of snow, God makes both rain and snow yield peace and joy in our lives. Isn't it hard though to hang onto that promise in the dead of winter? When we feel God has taken a vacation and left us in -10 degree weather? It doesn't seem fair.

Read Isaiah 55 and write out Isaiah 55:13:

Thorn bushes and briers grow because of un-cultivation. They are basically weeds. Junipers and myrtles are both evergreens—bushes and trees that are not only alive in the winter, but actually produce fruit in the winter.

Wow. Fruit in the winter? Cold temperatures and snow actually produce something summer and rain never could. This is why God speaks like rain. And it's also why He knows that sometimes His words need to be like snow.

Has God been planting seeds in your life that are meant to flourish in the wintery silence God sometimes leads us in?

In seasons of waiting, silence can be discouraging. But, as the Lord grows us into maturing believers, He teaches us to have faith and to believe in His words during all seasons of life.

When I experience silence, opening up the Word is so important to feed my soul with truth. As I read His promises, they begin accumulating in my soul like snowflakes do upon the ground.

live deeper

Has there been a time where you believed God was silent? What emotions did you experience as a result?

Yes, sadness and hopeless.

Look up Isaiah 55:8-9. These verses are about seasons of rain and seasons of snow in your spiritual life. How can you apply these verses to God's choice in how to speak to you in certain seasons?

That there are ^negatives thoughts, belief
that ^for god is not the same.

What does Proverbs 3:1-2 say? What do these verses instruct us to do that's helpful in seasons of snow?

to remember his teachings and
keep his commands regardless
of the season

reflection

Think about a season where God's words were like snow.
Was there fruit produced in your life because of the silence?
Ask God why He chose snow over rain in that season of life.

Yes .

God, Your thoughts are so different than mine! But that is
why You are God and I am not. Thank you for different
ways of how You speak. Please help me to endure the
snowy seasons with You, so I can rejoice in the peace You
bring. Amen.

learning to listen in the wait

As I was writing these words, God was actively teaching me about listening to Him and for Him in the wait. He also expanded my view of waiting! Waiting isn't just reserved for big life seasons. Waiting can also be on a smaller scale, with a definite and known end date. For me, my small waiting season was waiting for creative sparks to show up so that words could be written down on a piece of paper.

Do you have any "small" seasons of waiting going on within your "big" wait?

Well, ironically, or actually, not surprisingly, during the writing process for this study, God asked me to do *exactly* what I was writing about. He asked me to wait expectantly for Him to show up, for the words to show up. I remember one conversation in particular, where God's words whispered gently in my spirit:

God, I have no more words to write.

Just wait. They'll come.

But God, the deadline is in three days!

Enjoy the next two days with friends.

What? God, that seems REALLY irresponsible!

Do you not trust Me to pull through on the third day?

...It just doesn't seem *logical.* I have a lot to do!

I know. But you can trust Me. Enjoy these next two days with your friends.

Gulp. So I did. God knew I needed those conversations with my friends. They brought inspiration, rejuvenation, laughter, and love into my life when I needed it most.

Friend, we have learned together this week. God sometimes asks us to do illogical things in our waiting seasons. Through it, we build trust and confidence in His voice, His character, His love, and His grace. We learn to listen and obey. We may question along the way—there is no doubt about it. But our God is with us. He is our Ultimate Guide, leading the way for us to live life to its fullest.

What did you learn this week?
What was your biggest take away?

· To listen, talk to god and accept

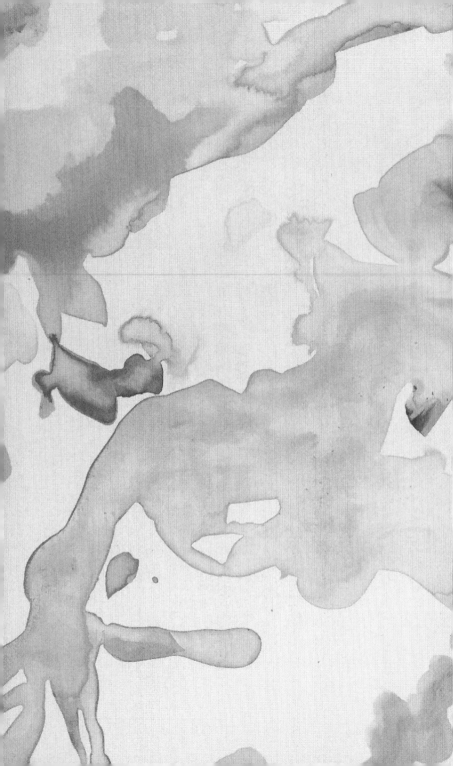

perseverance in the wait

Waiting is hard. Understatement of the year, perhaps? Often one of the toughest things about the wait is the multitude of unknowns. In seasons of waiting, questions can buzz around your head like a fly that presumptuously welcomed itself into your home. *What is going on? When will this be over? Why is this happening?* The minute the noise stops and you think the fly is gone, it starts up again. More buzzing. More questions. More unknowns. Shoo fly, I beg you to please stop bothering me.

After receiving some news about my dad's health that would change life as I knew it, my mind immediately went into high gear. I wanted to do something. Anything to make it better. I didn't have answers to my questions, and I allowed the unknowns to consume me as I tried to shut down the part of my soul that knew I needed to keep pressing on. The buzzing would go away if I just covered my ears, right?

49

Well, it didn't. But thankfully by God's grace, I began learning how to wait. And not just idle waiting, but waiting with perseverance. The kind of waiting that requires me to take steps forward even though I may feel like I have giant cement blocks permanently glued to my feet. Although I don't have the answers, I do know that God is calling me to keep going with grit and determination. He calls all of His followers to do the same. To persevere in seasons of waiting.

prepare your heart for the week

What thoughts or emotions does the phrase "perseverance in the wait" bring up for you? What lessons in perseverance do you hope to learn this week?

Holding on.
How perseverance help us.

facing difficulties

Blessed is the one who perseveres under trial because,
having stood the test, that person will receive the crown of
life that the Lord has promised to those who love him.
JAMES 1:12 (NIV)

I remember the moment I found out my dad had cancer like it was yesterday. I was sitting at work when my cell phone rang. It was my mom. I couldn't believe the words she was saying. After I made plans to go to the hospital where my dad was being prepped for emergency surgery, I went to tell my boss about the news I had just heard. I could barely get a few shaky words out of my mouth before the flood of tears began streaming down my face. Thoughts flitted through my mind saying that this couldn't possibly be real. Yet somehow it was.

I began to slip into a state of denial. Our family served a God who could do miracles, so God would surely heal my dad, wouldn't He? My father, a man who spent his life loving God and others. The kindest, most faithful man I've ever known. *Yes*, I thought, *God must be planning to save my dad and our family from the pain and heartbreak that normally comes with a diagnosis like this.*

With the hope I was holding on to, others began to assume I was handling everything remarkably well. Comments like "I don't know how you do it," were often directed my way. Even though the world I knew was crumbling before my eyes, it appeared on all fronts that I had it together. But on the inside, nearly all my energy was spent trying to deny any feeling of sadness or pain when I thought about the very real possibility of losing my dad. I couldn't bear it, so I did my best to overlook it.

After over a year of ignoring the truth about the situation, I began to face reality. It was time to take hold of this season of difficulty as opposed to letting it take hold of me. Then in September of 2012, my dad left this broken world, and he was made whole again as he went to his perfect, eternal home. My dad was healed.

We've all come face to face with difficulties. Maybe it was a job loss, a tough breakup, or an illness you didn't know how to manage. Maybe it was watching your parents' lifelong commitment to one another end in divorce, and years later, finding your own marriage headed in the same direction. Maybe it was an addiction, an eating disorder, or losing someone you couldn't imagine your life without.

Maybe it was desiring nothing more than to bring new life into the world and then being hit with an infertility diagnosis. Maybe it was watching your kids begin to stray from everything you worked so hard to teach them. Whether some of your most challenging moments thus far are behind you, or you are in the midst of dealing with them head on, rest assured that you are not in this fight alone.

Daniel of the Old Testament also had his share of difficulties during seasons of waiting. Daniel was an Israelite, and from all accounts, we can tell he lived a God-honoring life. Yet one day, he was taken into captivity and chosen to become a servant to the king of Babylon.

Take a look at part of Daniel's story in Daniel 1:1-6. How do you think Daniel felt as he was taken captive?

Can you imagine being taken from your home and your family? Nearly all you knew was suddenly changing—including your name?! And as if that's not enough, you're being forced to serve a king who could probably care less about you and the God you worship? Talk about depressing!

Everything around Daniel may have looked like it was ripping at the seams. Daniel could have crumbled. He could have given up and given in. Many probably wouldn't have even faulted him for it. He could have stopped waiting on God and gone into denial about his current situation. But he didn't. Daniel chose to keep moving forward even though he probably knew nothing about the grand plan God was knitting together for his life.

Daniel is arguably one of the most well-known and admired Old Testament characters because he persevered. He didn't give up when things looked like they had come crashing down around him. His life wasn't easy, but he kept moving despite the trials, and God honored Daniel and blessed his life greatly.

From Daniel's example, what can you apply to your own season of waiting?

God was with Daniel, and He is with us, too. He is on our side and will neither leave us nor forsake us. He wants to provide us with the wisdom and strength we need to successfully continue on and persevere in the midst of hardship. He promises that those who do this, who face into their difficulties instead of running the other way, will be blessed.

dive deeper

Spend a few minutes meditating on the words in James 1:5-8, 12. Would you describe yourself as one who keeps going even when it's tough? Do you think God sees you as a person who perseveres under trial?

Before No but now Yes.

What do these verses tell us about facing difficulties?

Isaiah 41:13   *Do not fear as god will help you*

John 16:31-33   *Take heart*

1 Peter 5:7   *Cast all your anxiety on him because he cares for you*

reflection

Have you ever felt like you didn't have what you needed in order to face a difficult situation? What is one thing you wish you had more of so you could handle these situations more effectively? Read Philippians 4:6-7, and ask God for what you need in order to get through whatever hardships you are facing today.

Yes. Faith and trust

Dear God, thank you for being my mighty and loving Father. I trust that You are fully able to provide me with what I need to navigate through difficulties. Help me to look to You for guidance while persevering through trials. Amen.

"- Trust yourself"
- 1/8/19

seizing opportunity

Not only so, but we also glory in our sufferings, because we know that suffering produces perseverance; perseverance, character; and character, hope.
ROMANS 5:3-4 (NIV)

The word *wait* in verb form can be defined as follows: to stay in place until an expected event happens; to remain stationary (Merriam-Webster, 2015). *Wait* can also be defined this way: to look forward expectantly; to be ready and available. Oftentimes, it seems like nothing can be accomplished during the wait, and if we think of waiting as a time to "remain stationary", no wonder we feel bored, helpless, and stuck.

There are certainly situations we cannot change, and waiting always seems to offer some new lesson in patience.

But what if we put patience into action as we offer ourselves to God, ready and available to what He may want to use us for and teach us during this time? What if we all started thinking of seasons of waiting as opportunities for growth? This thought pattern can take the seemingly mundane task of waiting and transform it into something more exhilarating than you ever imagined.

A phrase I've started using recently is "waiting well". Waiting well requires a number of things, but one piece that is an absolute necessity is noticing the opportunities that come about during the wait. And not just noticing them, but taking hold of them. Seizing the day, if you will.

After losing my dad, I was surrounded with opportunities to become closer to my family. I would have described us as tightly knit before, but now my family makes up my closest circle of friends. I tell them just about anything (probably more than they want to know at times!). My faith also grew in a significant way during this season. I never quite understood what it truly meant to "cry out to God" until going through some of my darkest, most painful moments of sorrow. This season brought up questions I never knew I had, but I came out stronger because of it.

Currently, my husband and I are waiting for our own family to grow. Ah yes, another intense season of waiting. As difficult as the last couple of years have been, I've come across many amazing opportunities. I've had time to invest in a job where I get to use my passions every single day. My husband and I have been able to focus on strengthening our marriage, and it's never been better. I have reconnected with old friends and met new friends—seriously, I feel like I've struck gold in the friendship arena. And to top it all off, I've been learning how to use my story as an encouragement for others.

So, what's the bottom line? Well, I still miss my dad and this infertility business is still hard, but I'm incredibly thankful for what has come from these struggles. There are certainly opportunities that have slipped by me on a bad day— probably more than I'd like to count. However, I am thankful that God has helped me take advantage of many of the blessings He's placed in my life.

Seeing the blessings God has put in your corner and seizing opportunities as they arise is a game changer. It can help you get from point A to point B as a better, stronger, more capable version of yourself. And yes, this is still true even if you don't know where point B is, what it will look like, or when you'll arrive.

According to James 1:2-4, what does the testing of faith produce?

Let perseverance finish it work so that you may be mature and complete, not lacking anything.

We've all suffered, faced trials, and had to wait for answers. When we persevere through those times, we're not just giving in and giving up. Choosing perseverance creates an opportunity to fight. A chance to exercise our faith muscles.

Perseverance not only allows us the opportunity to work on our right hook, but it also increases our character, and that character leads to hope (Romans 5:3-4). If we're being honest, most of us could benefit from some character reshaping along with a large deposit to fill our hope tanks. At least I know I could.

Read Daniel 6:1-4. Daniel didn't just sit around eating bonbons while he was in captivity. What did he do?

Although Daniel was forced into a season of service and waiting, he took hold of the opportunity to reach others. And not only did Daniel inspire and lead others thousands of years ago, his legacy has continued on, and his story is still reaching and encouraging multitudes of people this very day.

God did not create us to have boring, let's-just-sit-on-the-sidelines kinds of lives. He designed us in complex and amazing ways, and He wants us to live life to its fullest and seize the opportunities in front of us, even in our seasons of waiting.

live deeper

Luke 11:9 (NASB) says, "So I say to you, ask, and it will be given to you; seek, and you will find; knock, and it will be opened to you." Are you taking the opportunity to live out what Luke 11:9 instructs us to do during this season? Why or why not?

Yes,

Read Romans 5:3-5 and write out verse 5. Describe how you've seen perseverance lead to character and hope in your life or in the lives of those around you.

And hope does not put us to shame, bcoz god's love has been poured into our hearts through the Holy Spirit who has been given us.

reflection

Daniel didn't give up when he was taken into captivity.
Instead, he found ways to stand for his faith and lead others
in the process. How can you take a stand for your beliefs
during your times of wait? Think about some opportunities
you may have during your current season. Pray and ask God
to give you the strength to seize the day.

Dear God, You are the Giver of all things good. I thank you
for presenting me with opportunities to grow in character.
Open my eyes to what You want to teach me. Remind me
to use seasons of waiting to bring honor to You. Amen.

be brave

Have I not commanded you? Be strong and courageous. Do not be afraid; do not be discouraged, for the Lord your God will be with you wherever you go.
JOSHUA 1:9 (NIV)

The unknown is scary. Imagine floating around in the middle of outer space. Dark and lonely. Zero gravity and no direction. Meteors full of worries and insecurities propelling toward you. No idea where things begin and where or if they end. That's what the unknown can feel like if we're not anchoring ourselves in the gravitational pull of truth. And yeah, I'd say that's scary.

After my dad left this earth, I was afraid. I was scared of what life would be like without one of my greatest role models to call when I needed advice. Scared that our future children wouldn't know anything about their grandpa. Worried about what would happen to our family with our spiritual, moral, and emotional rock being taken away. And I was afraid of a whole lot of other things that would take up way too many lines (maybe pages) if I actually wrote them all out.

But I'm not so scared anymore. My dad would have wanted me to be brave. And more importantly, my God *created* me to be brave. In fact, He commands me and each one of His children to be both perseverant and brave.

The words in 2 Timothy 1:7 shed some truth and light on how God created us. Write that verse out and speak the words out loud.

The spirit god gave us does not make us afraid. His spirit is a source of power and love and self-control

God didn't create us with a spirit of fear or timidity. No way. He created us to be bold and to continue on even when we feel like turning in our badges. You, yes YOU, were made to be brave.

Being confident that we were made to be brave is a critical step, but in order to keep pushing ahead without letting fear creep into the cracks, we also need to uncover our values. Why? So we know what we're fighting for. Face it—it's easy to give up if you don't fully understand and believe in what you're doing. I have concluded that I value many things, but my primary values include my family, my friends, and above all, my Lord.

What are your primary values?

my spuse, my Lord, my family, my friends.

To honor our values, we need to make the choice to persevere even in the toughest moments. And you know what? I think persevering when we're wounded, tired, or just plain scared is one of the bravest things we can do.

Read Matthew 6:25-34. God knows that fear, worry, and anxiety are all part of being human in our fallen world. Yet, His Word says, "Do not worry about tomorrow." Easier said than done, right? I'm with you, but let's not forget that God knows us more intimately than we know ourselves. The same God who created the universe has whatever is causing your sleepless nights and sweaty palms under control. I believe that knowing this truth has the power to help us all begin to replace our hidden anxiety with in-your-face bravery.

Let's think back to Daniel and read Daniel 1:8-21. How did Daniel's actions require bravery?

He stood up to what he believe

In choosing not to defile himself by eating the king's food, Daniel honored God and remained true to his values. He boldly stood up for what he knew to be right. The Bible doesn't go into detail about any of Daniel's potentially hidden emotions. Did he experience fear? Did he feel any anxiety? I am guessing there was some of that mixed in there because, well, he was human, too. The important thing is that in Daniel's case, bravery won.

Daniel's example of boldness may seem small, but in that day and with the stakes he was facing, it wasn't. Daniel not only pleased the Lord, but his actions helped propel his entire career allowing him to witness to some of the biggest leaders of his day.

Daniel's brave act is just one of many outlined in the Bible. David, a young shepherd boy, went face to face with a giant with only a sling and some stones. Esther, a newly crowned queen, bravely risked her own life to help save her people. Paul, a former persecutor of Christians, began following Jesus and unapologetically proclaimed truth, knowing that he himself would be persecuted for it. These examples, as well as the many brave individuals around us today, will hopefully be an encouragement as we strive to boldly continue on during the wait.

live deeper

Being brave isn't often our natural inclination, especially as we grow older and see all of the heartache and pain in the world around us. However, we were made to be brave. Read the following verses and write out key words or phrases:

Deuteronomy 31:6

Be strong and brave

Joshua 1:9

The lord your god will be with you wherever you go

Isaiah 35:4

Isaiah 41:10

Dont worry - I am w/ you
Dont be affraid - I am your god

What do these four verses have in common in regards to God's promises?

reflection

How can believing the truth of God's promises change how we handle fears and anxieties? Think about the uncertainties you are currently facing. Be still, listen for God's voice, and allow His Spirit to move in you. What is He saying to you regarding the unknowns?

Dear God, You know the unknowns. Thank you that You will never leave me. Help me to truly hand my anxieties over to You, and remind me to seek You for the strength to be brave and courageous. Amen.

hold steady

Let us not become weary of doing good, for at the proper time, we will reap a harvest if we do not give up.
GALATIANS 6:9 (NLT)

Are we there yet?

Does this phrase strike a chord with anyone else? As a kid, I always wanted answers. *When are we going to the park? When will we get to open presents? When will I be old enough to color my hair and wear perfume?* You'd think I'd grow out of it, but as an adult, I still want an answer to the question, "Are we there yet?" I may actually ask myself those four words even more today than I did years ago while sitting in the backseat of my parents' Dodge Caravan. However, the questions taking over most of my thoughts these days, seem to be on a different scale than the wonderings I had as a tot. *When will the grief dissipate?* *When will we be able to grow our family? When will all of these hardships make more sense?*

When you've been waiting on something for any extended period of time, exhaustion undoubtedly tends to set in. You begin to lose critical perspective. It's like you're living in one big blur of questions and mystery. When this happens, we risk forgetting why we even took on this battle in the first place. Let me remind us of at least one really good reason to continue to hold steady and persevere: God keeps His promises.

What does Romans 8:28 tell us about those who love God?

We can find peace in knowing that God works for the good of those who have been called according to His purpose. God, the loving, powerful, omniscient Creator of the universe, works for our good if we truly love Him. And that's a promise.

Before you continue reading, pause and take a moment to think about what's making you weary today. It might be looking for that new job, car, church, or house. No matter how much you look, nothing seems to make sense. Maybe it's kids that won't behave even though you tried every trick in the book. It could be simply that despite how hard you try to keep your home and landscaping in presentable condition, it still seems to fall short. Who has time to pull weeds anyway?

No matter what you're facing today, you'd probably like to have the answers to a few of your top "when" questions. I wish I had a good piece of advice to offer, but unfortunately it's not that easy. We may not have the answers, but God does. This is why He calls us to hold steady in our trials—no matter how big or small.

Let's look at another part of Daniel's story by reading Daniel 6:1-18. Describe how Daniel chose to be obedient and hold steady despite his circumstances.

Daniel prayed each day during his season of servanthood and waiting, and he wasn't about to let fear of the unknown stop him from communing with God. Daniel may have felt weary. He may have thought that it'd just be easier to conform to the world around him. But he chose to hold steady. Daniel's decision led him to being forced to wait an entire night in a den full of lions. Now, one night may not seem like a long time to most of us who are in seasons of waiting, but just imagine the circumstances. Sitting right next to hungry, ferocious lions? Yikes!

Check out what happens next in the story by reading Daniel 6:19-28. How did God work good through Daniel's obedience and time of waiting in the lions' den?

Daniel's obedience and trust in God was rewarded. God not only saved Daniel from the lions' den, but He also used Daniel's story to show the truth about who God is to an entire kingdom. Daniel is an excellent example of what it looks like to stand firm in your beliefs despite opposition and demonstrate a genuine devotion to God.

Even when we know the truth about God's promises, waiting can still be hard because, face it, we're human. Waiting can range anywhere from mildly annoying to excruciatingly painful, but no matter where you are on the waiting spectrum, it's absolutely critical to hold steady.

Ecclesiastes 3:2 (NLT) says there is "a time to plant and a time to harvest." If you are in a season when all you feel like you're doing is planting, remember that the harvest is coming. And the more seeds you sow, the more blessings you will reap.

I want to share one additional thought with you about the importance of holding steady. Have you ever noticed that people are often the most tempted to quit right before a breakthrough? I believe this happens because there is an evil one who desperately wants to keep you from experiencing God's best for you. And evil seems to fight the hardest when we're on the verge of something incredible. Don't let evil win by stopping short of what God is doing! If we do, we're in danger of missing out on some of the greatest blessings we could ever experience.

dive deeper

In the book of Ecclesiastes, the author writes that there is a time for everything. Read Ecclesiastes 3:4-5. Do any of those times resonate with you? Why or why not?

Create your own "Time for Everything" list keeping in mind past or current seasons of waiting.

Read Matthew 11:28. What is making you weary today?

reflection

How can you use God's promises to ensure that you will not grow weary and stop short of what God is doing in your life? Meditate on Galatians 6:9 and Romans 8:28. Ask God to help you persevere as you trust in His commitments to His followers.

Dear God, thank you for the promises You have made to Your children. When I feel weak, I know You alone can make me strong. Help me remember I can hold steady and persevere with You by my side. Amen.

hoping eternally

Therefore, since we are surrounded by such a great cloud of witnesses, let us throw off everything that hinders and the sin that so easily entangles. And let us run with perseverance the race marked out for us.
HEBREWS 12:1 (NIV)

Whenever I read Hebrews 12:1, I am reminded of the day we celebrated my dad's life. This verse was the focus of the message from our family's beloved pastor of over twenty years. He preached this truth as hundreds sat, listened, and let reality sink in.

I couldn't have imagined any words more fitting for that day. A day marked with tears of love and of pain, feelings of hope and of sorrow, and a glimpse of heavenly light coming from the ashes. The juxtaposition of it all was almost too much for my brain to process. It was as if despair and holy anticipation were coming together to make a hauntingly beautiful symphony.

Hebrews 12:1 (NIV) begins by stating that we are "surrounded by a great cloud of witnesses." So who is this cloud of witnesses? Many believe it's those who have gone before us. Those who loved the Lord and ran the race here on earth until God called them home.

I don't know what heaven is like or how it works once you arrive, but if my dad is looking down on me from that cloud of witnesses, I want to make him proud. If amazing characters of faith like Daniel are watching, I want them to be cheering me on. But most importantly, I want to honor my Lord who I know is watching me every moment. And not only is He watching, He is by my side. And He is by yours too if you have chosen to follow Him and believe in the death and resurrection of His Son, Jesus.

But what about all of this waiting in the meantime? Waiting can easily drain us. It can zap every last bit of energy we possess with the worries, questions, and fears that hold our minds captive. It can make us feel like we are utterly incapable of taking another step forward. Waiting can blur our vision and allow us to get caught in a web of sin. There is good news though: it doesn't have to.

Read Romans 8:31-39, and write out verse 37.

Because of what Jesus did for us on the cross, we are more than conquerors. When our faith is in Christ, we can be sure that our biggest battle has already been won. Did you get that? Christ has *already* won! But that doesn't mean our work on earth is complete. God placed you here for a reason, for a purpose. Don't let the waiting and the unknown hinder you from completing your race. If God is for you, who can be against you? Answer: NO ONE.

2 Timothy 4:7 (NASB) reads, "I have fought the good fight, I have finished the course, I have kept the faith." I love those words, but they are actually pretty intimidating when you think about what they mean. It's a good kind of intimidating though. A kind of intimidation that drives you to be the person God created you to be. And we are not in this alone with only our broken selves to rely on either.

What does 1 Corinthians 3:16 say about God's people?

God's Spirit lives in those who have put their faith in Christ. We are not alone! Knowing that truth makes 2 Timothy 4:7 actually attainable. God calls us to live our lives in such a way so that at the end of our race, we can be confident that we ran with perseverance. And He will help us do just that!

No matter where you're at in your race, it's not too late to tighten the laces on your running shoes. Even if you are still stretching at the starting line or if you've paused midway through the course for a long drink of water, God wants you to know that you can get back on track today. I want to live a "2 Timothy 4:7" kind of life, and I pray that you do too.

We can start this very moment. Let's run the race He marked out for us!

live deeper

Read Romans 8:37 again. Write out the answer to the
following question in big, bold letters: Because of the One
who loves us, what are we more than?

Write out key words or phrases from Romans 8:38-39. Let
the reality of those words flow over and through you.

We can be confident that there is a cloud of witnesses surrounding us (Hebrews 12:1). What are you to throw off and leave behind so that you can finish your race with perseverance?

How can you be confident that God will help you finish your race well? (Deuteronomy 31:6, Isaiah 41:13)

Dear God, You are the Lord over all. You created heaven and Earth, and yet, You care about me. Remind me to throw off all that hinders and to run the race You've marked out for me. Help me to keep the faith every day. Amen.

learning to persevere in the wait

Through reflecting on my own ability to persevere during the wait, I am reminded both of how far I have come as well as how far I have yet to go. No matter how much I grow in my ability to hold steady and keep going through the challenging times, I need to constantly remind myself about God's goodness, His commands, and His promises. I need Him in the wait.

So how can we honor God as we wait? We cannot forget that even in seasons of waiting, the race is still going. Although we need to pause, reflect, and be still from time to time, we must remember that our course isn't done until God calls us home. So what are you waiting for? On your mark, get set, go!

What's something new you learned this week? What was a good reminder? What surprised you about God? About yourself?

- waiting well.
- perseverance nature

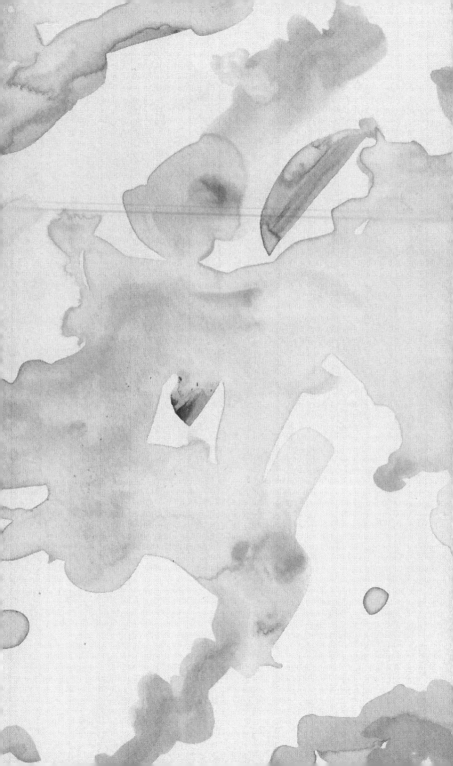

community in the wait

Shortly into our newlywed life, my husband became incredibly ill, and my vision for a comfortable life was shattered into a million pieces, full of unanswered questions as sharp and painful as broken glass. We weren't expecting a chronic diagnosis. *When will he heal? What if he doesn't heal? Why do I feel so incredibly alone? How long will we be in this isolating season?*

With each passing month, the loneliness sank into my heart and burrowed down deep into my soul. Our closest friends and family were separated from us by hundreds of miles, and I tried to carry the impossible weight of the world by holding our life together on my own.

Through the dark, truth began to emerge like a rainbow after a frightening storm—I am not alone in the waiting. We all are created for community.

prepare your heart for the week

What do you hope to learn about community this week? Be honest and open, asking the Lord what He wants you to glean.

To be out spoken & communicate with him

discovering identity

For you created my inmost being; you knit me together in my mother's womb. I praise you because I am fearfully and wonderfully made...
PSALM 139:13-14a (NIV)

The days spent in the hospital passed by slowly and incredibly fast all at the same time. It seemed like we were living an out-of-body experience. Test upon test and no sure answers left my mind wondering what our life was becoming.

Depression had set in as black as night, and all sight of my identity was lost in the brokenness of our present circumstances. *What do we do now? Is this our reality? Will we be defined by this season forever?* All my hopes for our future—financial peace, a growing family, and a healthy husband—were shattered in an instant. Suddenly, I couldn't clearly see who I was or what our future looked like anymore.

Have you ever had a season like this? Perhaps your identity was lost in the desperation of finding a job, impending divorce papers, or worrying if your parenting was enough. We take on these labels—unemployed, divorced, bad parent—and forget that these labels do not define us!

Sometimes all we can see is a big black hole with only the negatives and difficulties staring back at us. We can seek comfort in all the wrong places. Although we know our identity is found in Christ, we crave something tangible to fill the God-sized void in our hearts. The labels begin to tell us lies...

You are not strong enough to overcome this struggle.
You are not good enough to make it to the other side.
You are not patient enough to live through the wait.
You are not enough...
You are not enough...

These words repeat in our head so often that we begin to believe them. The lies seep into our soul, steal our joy, and transform our identity into something completely unrecognizable. Our identities slowly can become defined by the lies of "not enough" rather than the truth.

Do you ever feel as though you are not enough? When does this lie show up the most?

Read 1 Peter 2:9-10. What truth does this verse proclaim over our lives?

Our true identity is written all throughout the Scriptures. It can be so easy during seasons of hardship to be overwhelmed by a false sense of self, so let's dig in deep to the truth. We are daughters of Christ, created in the image of God, fearfully and wonderfully made, redeemed and forgiven, a masterpiece, chosen by God. As Christians, our identity is rooted in Him and nothing we do changes that.

Throwing off the lies and incorrect labels of this world allows us to see ourselves through God's lens. In Him we have been given a new life to embrace each and every day.

As we begin to claim our identity in Christ alone, the burden of the waiting season shrinks away. Yes, we still might be carrying a heavy load and our struggles won't necessarily be removed in an instant, but the choice to place our full faith and identity in God's unfailing hands saves us from despair.

God knew us before we were even formed. He numbered our days giving each one a purpose. Even if we are in the dark, we can still see the light because He is the Light of the World. In Him, we find our true identity.

dive deeper

How do you view yourself? How do you think God sees you?

Let's take time to dive a little deeper into the truths we have learned today. As you are reading these verses, write out keywords that fill you up with encouragement.

Genesis 1:27

Psalm 139:14

Isaiah 43:1

Ephesians 1:7

Ephesians 2:10

reflection

Where are you seeking your identity? In relationships, things of this world, in Christ, or in something or someone else?

Dear Lord, thank you for reminding me over and over that my identity is found in You. Thank you for loving me even when I run the opposite direction. Help me to remember that You are always there for me through it all. Amen.

freedom from loneliness

Cast all your anxiety on him because he cares for you.
1 PETER 5:7 (NIV)

The months passed and the weather changed, but the season of our life remained as cold and as lonely as before. Carrying the weight of my husband's chronic illness, I found myself on numerous occasions staring blankly at my phone wanting desperately to call a friend, but not knowing where to start or how to ask for help. How do you explain the depths of sadness to someone else when you don't even know how to put it into words yourself?

We found ourselves in a seemingly unending season of waiting and transition, searching for healing and support. Slowly, brick by brick, the walls of my heart went up. Our close friends and family were miles away, and I realized we did not have any local community.

Have you ever seen the show *Friends*? Maybe you have read the book *7* by Jen Hatmaker or *Bread and Wine* by Shauna Niequist. There is a reason why this show and these books are so popular—the relationships in them are evident.

As much as we crave community with the Lord and others, sometimes we can't figure out how to break free from the loneliness that holds us in captivity. When we don't have the strength to reach outside of our own sphere of hardships, we wait for friendship to fall into our laps. When that doesn't happen, incredible loneliness can fill our hearts.

Countless times, I cried out to God as David did in the Psalms. It's inspiring that someone called a man after God's own heart (1 Samuel 13:14) felt as lonely and distant as I did. Psalm 141:1 in *The Message* perfectly captures the despair that we sometimes feel when swallowed up by seasons of waiting and hardship. "God, come close. Come quickly! Open your ears—it's my voice you are hearing!"

Think back on a time where you have felt lonely, overwhelmed by life's circumstances. Read Psalm 139:7-12. What does this passage tell us about the presence of God?

That his spirit is everywhere I go.

Something happens to us in the middle of seasons of waiting or hardship. It forces us to face our fears and decide what's truly important. God is the One who knew us before we were created. We have a choice: will we turn to Him or will we flee?

During that time in my life, tears came to my eyes every time *Oceans* by Hillsong played on the radio or blared through our living room speakers.

"Spirit, lead me where my trust is without borders.
Let me walk upon the water wherever You would call me."

As I sang those words and prayed, I had no idea what journey would lie ahead. I was forced to turn to Him with my whole heart.

"Take me deeper than my feet could ever wander and
my faith will be made stronger in the presence of my Savior."

As a result, when I turned to Him, my faith became stronger. Psalm 9:9-10 (MSG) says, "God's a safe-house for the battered, a sanctuary during bad times. The moment you arrive, you relax; you're never sorry you knocked." Wow, imagine letting go of the anxiety that is filling your life while waiting and embracing the unfailing peace of being in the "safe-house" of the Lord.

Think of what you are waiting for today: that fresh start, a place to finally call home, a car that will take you safely to work, meaningful friendships with people who genuinely care about you. Are you willing to let go of the fears that surround you to embrace God's hope and peace?

When I came to the realization that my broken self could have community with the Lord no matter what state my life was in, I chose to run into His open arms. Prayer became honest and vulnerable, less about formalities or rituals. Scripture came pouring out of my pen and paper as I worshiped in the only way I knew how, through art.

How do you connect with the Lord? Worship is so much more than saying an awkward prayer. Be still. Embrace the quiet. Take a walk around your neighborhood, turn on a worship album while getting ready for the day, create a new painting, write in a journal, study Scripture—the sky's the limit! It's not about having the perfect quiet time ritual, but rather spending time with God and trusting that He will make beauty from the shattered pieces of our life.

We have to invest in our relationship with Christ in order to hear His whispers. Our Heavenly Father will never leave us. He has made a home for us so we can nestle into Him.

We long to see the plans that He set out for our lives. We want His perspective, but we can't always see how the circumstances of our lives are going to work out for our good. Even when we don't have all the answers, let's lean into the One who never fails us. When we choose to do this, our relationship with the Lord will blossom. In the good and bad times, God reveals Himself to us in new ways. He uses our seasons as an invitation to turn to Him for comfort, advice, and friendship.

No matter how far away we are or how lonely our current season is, God is always with us. We cannot flee from His presence. Let's us run into His open arms full of love and grace.

dive deeper

John 15:15 says that Jesus has called us friends. In what ways would you say He has revealed Himself to you as a friend?

Listen to the song *Come to Me* by Jenn Johnson. How do you feel after hearing this song? Did any of the words grab your attention and fill you with truth? Write them below as a reminder.

reflection

One of the most challenging things to do is lay aside our own desires to wholly focus on our relationship with the Lord. We want this season of waiting to be over, the uncertainty to end, and the relief to come. What would it look like to really cast these anxieties on the Lord in exchange for His peace?

Lord, thank you for being with us through it all.
Thank you for being our Healer, Guide, Friend, Protector, and Comforter. Help us to remember that even when we feel lonely, You are here for us. Remind us of Your truth. Amen.

finding community with others

...that there may be no division in the body, but that the members may have the same care for one another. If one member suffers, all suffer together; if one member is honored, all rejoice together. Now you are the body of Christ and individually members of it.

1 CORINTHIANS 12:25-27

Community with others looks different for everyone. Looking back over the last few years of my life, it's obvious that meaningful friendships are not created overnight. It takes time and hard work to invest in others' lives repeatedly, authentically, and genuinely in order to develop deep relationships.

Newly married and fresh out of the college scene, we planned on investing in a small group, having gatherings in our home, and getting to know the people in our neighborhood. Instead, we found ourselves in a hospital room, waiting for healing and relief. I was working two jobs, starting a business, caring for my husband, and attempting to manage the housework. No wonder I was unraveling at the seams!

Even though we had little to give, we chose to seek out intentional friendships and prayed that God would lead us into a strong community of believers. I started creating art again as I tried to discover God's purpose in our wait. As I started sharing my lettering and our journey on Instagram, an online community began to surround us. People we didn't know began praying for us and encouraging us daily to not give up hope. I was blown away! I learned the first step is letting people into our lives so they can get close enough to offer encouragement.

When trying to find a local small group, I came across an online network of community groups. *Yay! Maybe this is something I could do! Oh wait. I've missed the deadline for signing up.* At that point I had a choice to make: do I put myself out there by emailing someone I do not know to ask if it's really too late to join in or do nothing and continue to search for something else?

I chose to jump and asked if there was room for one more in any group. You know what? There was! Stepping outside of our comfort zones opens the doors to let community into our lives. It challenges us to seek out friendships rather than waiting for them to fall into our laps.

Taking that first leap of faith and emailing a stranger was extremely difficult for my shy, introverted self, but the leaps that came after were just as challenging. On the night of our first community group online meeting, I burst into tears out of fear that these women would be unwilling to meet me where I was. You know the feeling—butterflies in your stomach, minutes that feel like hours, the inevitable technical issues—the lies start flying! *It's sooooo obvious that this group isn't going to work because everything seems to be going wrong. Should I just give up?*

Have you ever felt this way? Did you ever want to give up because it seemed like every time you tried to make connections everything was working against you?

When we pour out our hearts and continue to seek ways to grow, we begin to see a glimpse of His hand orchestrating friendships that define what community is all about.

In Exodus 17, the Israelites were at war with Amalek, and God commanded Moses to keep his arms raised. As long as his arms were raised, Israel was winning the battle. Read Exodus 17:8-13. What did Aaron and Hur do for Moses?

When Moses' strength failed, Aaron and Hur helped him continue the battle for the Lord. One on each side, they kept Moses' arms held high and as a result the battle was won. This picture of community is so incredibly powerful. We all desire friends that will come alongside us no matter what and keep our arms held high in praise while we fight the battles that threaten to take the life right out of us.

We were created to be in community. In the beginning, God created a partner for man so he would not be alone (Genesis 1:27). God walked and talked with Adam and Eve who He created in His own likeness. The early church did everything together continuously. In fact, "[A]ll the believers lived in a wonderful harmony, holding everything in common. They sold whatever they owned and pooled their resources *so that each person's need was met*" (Acts 2:44-45 (MSG), emphasis mine). Isn't that amazing? The early church made a point to engage in the community, pull their resources together, and meet the needs of those around them.

Community is not limited to those who are next door, down the street, at church, or the PTA meeting. Community is everywhere. When we see a need, we are called to reach out and meet it. Will we make the choice to cross over into their story or ignore them and move on with our life? Will we share Christ's love no matter what the cost is for us? Will we be still? Listen? Administer mercy?

Friendships begin when one person takes the first step to get to know another, listening and working together to build a relationship. When we are able to do that for a friend, they can do the same for us. For me this became absolutely true. Discovering true community stirred a personal passion in me to encourage others in their seasons of waiting, loneliness, and hardship.

Loving one another in the context of community is a large part of our call as disciples of Jesus. He commanded us to love one another in Mark 12:30-31, and He did not just drop commands lightly! Jesus knows that we need each other. Both hard and happy times are ahead, and community is necessary to make it through both. True, deep friendships do not give up when the going gets tough. Instead, they continuously point us back to God, to the One who is full of love.

live deeper

When you think of deep friendships, who comes to mind? If you do not have a local community, pray and ask God for one person. Friendships are a gift. Cherish them. We were not created to live life alone (Ecclesiastes 4:9-10).

Do you long for meaningful relationships? Pray and ask God for one person you know and take the time to reach out to her.

reflection

What are some practical ways you can connect with other like-minded people? Make a list below and choose to take action on one! Here are a few ideas to get you started: join or start a small group, take a cooking class, participate in recreational sports, serve with someone to meet a need. If it challenges you to step outside your comfort zone, it's probably a good thing to try!

Jesus, thank you for showing us what living in community with others looks like. Guide us into intimate relationships that will draw us closer to You. Amen.

when life hurts

*Bear with each other and forgive one another if any
of you has a grievance against someone.
Forgive as the Lord forgave you.*
COLOSSIANS 3:13 (NIV)

During our most challenging days, I craved local community—someone to bring over a meal, stop by to check on us, enter into our mess full of love and grace. I did not understand why we were being asked to walk this journey without the support of friends nearby; so the walls of my heart went up, and it became near impossible to bring them down again.

Setting expectations of God and others can hinder us from living fully. When life isn't going according to our plans, or our dreams for the future are stripped away, it is easy to feel hurt.

God, why did this happen?
Why did You not stop it?
Why didn't You answer my prayers?

We easily find ourselves wallowing in the *why* and *what if* and forget that God has promised to keep us in perfect peace. He declares that He knows our future and will not fail us. If we really truly believe He is faithful, why is this promise so easy to forget?

Asking God *why* is perfectly normal; however, if this question pushes us farther from Him rather than drawing us closer, it is the wrong question to dwell on. Let's try refocusing the *why* to *what*.

Now that this is my situation, what am I supposed to do?
What can I learn from this?
What other opportunities could God be providing?

Take a moment to remember a recent experience where you asked God *why*. How can you shift the reflective *why* to the active *what* in your own life? In what ways may God be teaching, protecting, and providing for you?

As we face into the *what*, we recognize our need for others. Community was created as a blessing, but because of sin we mess up all the time. Sometimes our friends fail us and we can feel hurt when the people we expected to be there for us disappear. Likewise, we may not even realize how we may be hurting our own friends! Because we don't ask for what we need, our expectations can set us and our friendships up for failure.

Misunderstandings, frustrations, and hurt feelings happen all the time. We have to be willing to deal with the mess and fight for our friendships, not only looking at our needs but also the needs of others. So, reach out to one another. Bring a meal to a friend in need. Drop off a cup of coffee. Send a note of encouragement. One simple kind word or action can make a lasting impact.

Unfortunately, sometimes friends hurt us on purpose as well, but it's up to us to react in love and forgiveness, not in anger and revenge. The story of Joseph in Genesis shares a beautiful account of forgiveness against all odds.

In Genesis 37, most of Joseph's brothers betrayed him, sold him into slavery, and lied to their father about Joseph's death. They fully intended to hurt him all because they were jealous.

Now read Genesis 50:14-21. How did Joseph react to his brothers?

Imagine yourself in Joseph's place. How do you think you would have reacted?

Forgiveness is not letting an offender off the hook, but rather, returning the right to God to take care of justice. People still need to be held accountable for their actions. Joseph chose to forgive his brothers for their horrible actions toward him. He didn't seek revenge because he believed that God used for good what his brothers meant for evil.

Within community, we can always choose forgiveness.

dive deeper

What are the expectations you have of your community? Are they standing in your way of embracing true community?

Read Colossians 3:12-17. What are we to put on?

reflection

Forgiveness brings joy and peace! Is there a friendship you have let go of because it got messy? Ask God if this relationship is worth fighting for. If yes, what would an action step toward restoration look like for you today?

Father God, search my heart and help me to see if there is any bitterness within me. Heal my hurts, Lord, and help me to learn to trust in You always. Teach me to be still, to listen to other's needs, and to administer forgiveness always.
Amen.

contentment within community

"If I were writing my life story, it would have turned out differently..." The words hung in the air for what seemed like an eternity as the reality of what I just said sank in. As much as I wanted to, I couldn't take them back.

Was I really asking for my life to look different? Was I really declaring for all to hear that I did not trust God to write a beautiful story out of my life? Did I really believe that He wouldn't provide for me? I was discontent.

Sometimes we scroll through social media, and each post that goes by fuels the discontentment in our hearts. The internal voices sound like:

Wow, she has such a beautiful house. Will mine ever look so put together?
That looks so fun! But, why did she get to take a girls weekend away? My family is barely scraping by.
Another friend is pregnant? What is wrong with me? Why can't we pull our life together? It feels like everything is always falling apart.

Have you ever had thoughts like these? If yes, how has this hindered your ability to be content?

Sometimes the threat of comparison rips community apart before there is even an opportunity for friendship to begin. Social media can be a like seam ripper to the heart, blinding us to the blessings in our own life as we see the things everyone else seems to have. It's a classic case of "the grass is always greener on the other side."

As I mentioned earlier this week, social media and online community is a wonderful way to connect with like-minded individuals around the world or even right in your own neighborhood. Unfortunately, connecting through the internet only paints half a picture, disguising part of reality. We see the highlights of friends' lives and forget about the challenges they also face daily. Discontentment is not limited only to online relationships. It happens everywhere, even in our own neighborhoods.

In what areas of life are you struggling with discontentment? Does this hinder you from connecting in community with God or others?

Now that we have identified our areas of discontentment, how do we live a life of contentment? As we ponder this, let's reflect on a few principles:

Stop looking right or left, and choose to look up. When it comes to learning how to live in contentment, the best thing we can do is take our focus off the things of this world and place it on Christ.

Focus more on what you do have rather than what you don't have. Contentment has very little to do with getting what we want, but rather, appreciating what we have. Take a moment to look around at the things you have been given. Cultivating gratitude for the things we have is a choice.

Let go of the Shoulda, Coulda, and Woulda. We get stuck in this mindset and fixate on how things could possibly be different if we had only chosen a different path. In order to fully embrace contentment, we need to choose to keep looking forward.

Always remember, your story matters. The things you are going through have a purpose, whether you can see the whys or not. To quote Author Susie Larson: "He is writing a beautiful story with our lives. His will for us is our best-case scenario. He doesn't want us to want someone else's story, because ours fits us perfectly."

We only get a partial story from the tweets, news feeds, and looking at those around us, but even if it were the whole story, the truth is still the same to us—Christ is our true source of contentment.

live deeper

What discovering contentment principle sticks out to you the most? How can you apply it to your life?

Read Philippians 4:12 out loud, and write it below. Do you believe you can find true contentment in Christ?

reflection

Who or what are you comparing yourself to? Ask God how He wants you to become more content in these areas. If you need accountability, share your thoughts with a trusted friend.

Father God, help me to recognize the blessings that are in my life even when I cannot see them. I want to be overflowing with contentment and joy in all circumstances. In Your name, Amen.

finding community in the wait

No matter what life throws our way, we always have community in the Lord. He promises to never leave us or forsake us. This week, we discovered that every little step we take toward engaging in the community around us is like sowing seeds that in time will reap a harvest of friendship.

God is glorified when we live in harmony and care for one another. By dwelling in unity as the body of Christ, we reflect our Maker. Steve Gladden says, "We undertake the mission of God together because by God's design there is power in 'together'." We are able to meet other's needs and show God's love to the world when we are unified as the body of Christ.

More than anything, believe that no matter what you are facing, you are not alone in your wait. *You are not alone.*

What was your biggest takeaway from this week? Claim this truth and write it below.

joy in the wait

Always be joyful. Never stop praying.
Be thankful in all circumstances, for this is God's will
for you who belong to Christ Jesus.
1 THESSALONIANS 5:16-18

Did you catch the verse above? Go ahead, reread it.
Gulp. *Always* be joyful? Often times I feel like saying, "God,
waiting is one thing, but asking me to have JOY while
waiting is really pushing my limits." Yet, that statement isn't
as radical as it feels. In fact, we see it's something God
confirms throughout the Bible—be joyful no matter what our
circumstances are, regardless of what our waiting season is.

If you are anything like me, you may want to push off
the season of waiting. I've been waiting to become a mom

for quite a long time, but that prayer has not been answered yet, at least not with a baby in my arms. My season of waiting lingers on. It can keep me up at night, bring tears to my eyes on occasion, and drain me of what little strength I have. So joy in the waiting means work. Can you relate?

It doesn't have to be that way. In fact, it shouldn't be that way. There IS a way to handle trials and seasons of waiting with joy, the kind that keeps our hearts content and our perspectives upward. The solution? God has equipped us with ways to cultivate joy so that we don't have to feel depleted.

prepare your heart for the week

What do you expect to learn from this week's study? Be honest and open, asking the Lord what He wants you to take away.

The Joy of waiting

- dreamt mama preggy haha
1-22-19

overcoming shame and guilt

So if the Son sets you free, you will be free indeed.
JOHN 8:36

Waiting is hard. My husband and I have been waiting to grow our family for over six years and have faced more medical treatments, invasive surgeries, and miscarriages than I would have ever imagined. Waiting for something I feel like God has promised and not seeing that fulfilled is exhausting in every sense of the word. Do you know this feeling in your own story?

Have you ever looked at your trial, season, or time of waiting wondering if it's because of something you have done in the past? Sometimes I feel like this season is a punishment. My guilt and failures overwhelm me. I replay past forgiven sins and wonder which one has caused this? This question weighs heavily on my soul.

In Romans 3:23-24, God tells us we have all sinned and fallen short, but because of Jesus we have been forgiven. Our punishment has been taken away! I no longer need to carry guilt from the past. I'm given the freedom to embrace this season.

We have to make a decision to *always be joyful*. We can either get stuck in anger, guilt and shame, or we can accept His abundant gift of grace and forgiveness.

Waiting can be a beautiful time of refinement: a chance to grow closer to Jesus and for Him to change our perspective. But refinement can't happen if we allow ourselves to be held captive. The devil wants nothing more than to cut us off from the Father's heart, to try to get us to believe that these trials are a punishment.

Sin causes consequences, and our response to the Holy Spirit is important. But the beautiful thing is there is redemption when we confess our sins and turn from our ways. When we partner with the Lord, He offers us the freedom from carrying the burden of guilt and shame. Instead of being held captive to fear, we can see weaknesses as opportunities to blossom. In fact, Hebrews 12:8a (MSG) says clearly, "This trouble you're in isn't punishment, it's training, the normal experience of a Christian."

I am so thankful Jesus takes our shame from our shoulders and loves us regardless. I've messed up in big and small ways. I've battled with not forgiving myself, but I've learned thinking about the what-if's steals my joy. I need

God's help to accept the grace and forgiveness He's already offered me.

Are you like me at all? It can be easy when we face hardships to blame ourselves, believing maybe God hasn't really forgiven us. But when we believe that, we transform God's character into a Father who is vindictive, not one who wants the best for His children.

Let's look at some biblical examples. What words are used to describe Job in Job 1:1 and Zechariah and Elizabeth in Luke 1:6?

These verses bring me comfort because they show that even blameless and righteous servants of God share in suffering, too. In those moments where I am on my knees yet again, I am reminded God doesn't reward or withhold from my life based on what I deserve. (If it was that scenario, we'd all be in trouble!)

We find examples of God's grace and mercy throughout His Word. For me, knowing Elizabeth's barrenness wasn't without purpose brings me comfort. It wasn't a punishment God placed upon her but instead, an opportunity for her to become the mother of John the Baptist.

Do you believe that He may hold an opportunity for you as well? (Ephesians 3:20)

If you are feeling imprisoned by guilt and shame, worrying that God is withholding good things from you because of past sins, I encourage you to work through that with Him today. He is the only One capable of offering us the freedom and forgiveness we need. With His help, we can take this step to become women of true joy in this season.

live deeper

Write out 1 John 1:9 and reflect on His goodness.

Take time to reflect on God's character. Jot down characteristics of His heart that allow you to live in freedom from guilt and shame.

Lamentations 3:22-23

Psalm 30:5

Psalm 103:11-13

Psalm 145:17

Which verse sticks out to you the most? Take time to write out that verse (or another that has stuck out to you today) on an index card and place it where you can see it daily.

reflection

Take time to make your heart right with God and meditate on the fact that God does not wish for you to suffer. His compassion and love will flood our hearts if we allow them to and if we surrender the guilt and shame we secretly carry.

What action do you need to take to set your heart free from shame so that you're able to live a life of joy with the Lord? What is one area in which you need to be intentionally prayerful about releasing to God and accepting His forgiveness?

Lord, thank you for Your gift of grace and Your promise to forgive me. I offer up my heart to You today, asking You to give me the strength to forgive myself. Supply me with the power to believe that this wait is a gift to become more like You. Amen.

surviving tested faith

*For you know that when your faith is tested,
your endurance has a chance to grow.*
JAMES 1:3 (NLT)

In today's world, we see things all around us being tested—relationships, health, careers, plans for the future, and then ultimately, as a result, our faith. It happens so often, but when I'm tested, I'm still shocked. *But I am a good person, a Christ follower! This shouldn't be happening! I pray!* James 1:3 shares an eye-opener about tested faith in one little word— "when". *When,* not "if."

I have spent seasons of life wrestling with the fact that God isn't a genie. What I want to do is just offer up a prayer and have every hardship magically disappear. Why does life have to be so hard sometimes? What's even harder is believing God hears my prayers in this current season of suffering. My faith is tested when I feel ignored. But then His Word speaks truth into me ... *this is an opportunity to grow.*

It all sounds so good doesn't it? Truth is, it's really tough to embrace our faith when testing happens—jobs are lost abruptly, unexpected deaths occur, relationships end without notice. When shocking news hits us, *OH YAY!* isn't the first phrase that comes to mind.

We've all been there, haven't we? A time when we've had to endure one of those big life moments, knowing that the aftermath is going to change us. Have you ever wondered what the point was? Me too.

Read 1 Peter 1:6-7 (NLT). What sticks out to you about these verses in regard to trials?

These troubles test your faith is worth more than gold.

So we've added in another component. Not only do we know we have trials ahead to endure, but now we're told to be truly glad in the midst of it all. *Yikes!* The Bible shares that we have the freedom to rejoice in the hardships for a very specific reason—our faith is strengthened and God is glorified. If that's not a motivator to face into trials, I don't know what is!

When trials come—since it's clear that it's a matter of "when" not "if"—we have to ask ourselves what we are going to do with our attitudes and our hearts in the struggle.

Do you believe that it's possible to *really* be filled with joy? Why or why not?

Yes

In order to discover genuine joy, we have to remember that joy is not reliant on circumstances. Our joy is held together by the character of Jesus and the relationship we have with Him. Do we really believe He will never forsake us? We meditated on His character yesterday and saw He is full of goodness, compassion, mercy, love, and forgiveness. The Bible demonstrates that He has never failed His children in the past. He isn't going to start now and use us as the first example!

Sometimes our inner voice yells that He can't be trusted. I mean, it makes no sense for people to have to go through infertility or singleness or unemployment or anxiety for *this long*. He must have forgotten about us. But when emotions seems to be winning, faith steps in and shoves it out of the way. His Word wins over emotions. Because despite all our feelings, His peace is greater.

When we are burdened with sorrow, when we're crying out to Him, He meets us in that moment. He brings comfort to our hearts, and cradles us close. Those precious moments of tear-filled fellowship are among my favorite times with Him.

When the wait seems like it's never going to end and more hardships hit, let your knees buckle. Collapse into the open arms of Jesus who is waiting to hold us close. The grenades may still be exploding around us, but we are wrapped in the most protective arms possible.

The times in my life when I cry out, "I CAN'T TAKE IT ANY MORE!" are the valued moments where God whispers back, "You weren't supposed to "take it" to begin with."

Take a second to read through Matthew 11:28. Read it and then write it out in the space below. Finally, speak it out loud as if Jesus was physically present saying it to you. What words or phrases stick out to you?

I will give you rest.

You may be reading today thinking, *You just don't get it. My season is harder than most. It's just not possible.* But Friend, it IS, because of the simple fact that He is stronger. He will meet you on the floor. He will fill your heart with peace and joy. Being bitter is easy because it requires no fight. But becoming someone of godly character? Well, that's well worth the battle!

So how do we survive tested faith with joy? By leaning deeply into Him, by being truly glad for an opportunity to show our faith as genuine, and by trusting so deeply for others to see that He is glorified.

dive deeper

In Week 2, we studied Romans 5:3-5 as it talked about rejoicing in our sufferings. Let's review it for a moment: (ESV translation)

"Not only that, but we rejoice in our sufferings, knowing that:

troubles produces _patient_ →

Patience produces _strong_ →

strong produces _hope_ →

and _hope_ does not put us to _disappointment_.

Now reread verse 5. How is this made possible?

God has poured out his love fill our hearts through Holy Spirit he gave us.

When we remember our joy isn't based on our circumstances, our joy in Him increases. What can you do today to increase your joy?

Thankful and grateful for god's love .

reflection

It's challenging to identify how your wait is affecting your faith in a positive way. Take some time to reflect on how it's grown as a result of this season. Write down a prayer asking God to help mold your perspective to see Him more today.

Lord, thank you for the opportunity to become more like You. I don't always understand the plan, but I trust You. Help me to lean in today and every day, growing my faith and endurance. Gather me up in Your arms and take these burdens off my shoulders. I ask for Your joy to fill my heart. Amen.

practicing patience

Wait patiently for the Lord. Be brave and courageous.
Yes, wait patiently for the Lord.
PSALM 27:14 (NLT)

Growing up, I always thought my little sister was impatient. I remember a woman from church saying, "Patience can't be perfected, only practiced," and thinking, Yikes, she's got a ways to go. The joke seems to be on me many years later. I never thought I would be here learning so much about this small word. Yes, my life has required a bit of patience.

It's really hard to have to wait for something, isn't it? Merriam-Webster defines the word patience as "being able to remain calm and not becoming annoyed while waiting for a long time". After reading that, it's clear that I certainly do stumble at times with patience.

Romans 8:25 teaches us a valuable lesson about patience. What is it?

waiting patiently

The longer I wait, the more I realize how different my timeline is from His. Our world is filled with the conveniences of immediate gratification. Need coffee? Starbucks drive-thru. Want to watch a movie? Download from iTunes. Concerned about the dog's health? Google it.

And then there are the things that don't just happen overnight. The house is still on the market, Prince Charming hasn't showed up yet, career advancement seems bleak, or your toddler still isn't talking. How do we embrace these challenges?

I tend to want to rush through them. Can I manipulate the situation? What can I do to reach my end goal? I want to fast forward to the next season where things *have* to be better than they are now, right? Ever been there?

We can forget that patience is a major characteristic of God. Trials give us an opportunity to become more like Him, and yet, if you're like me at all, we can want to push those lessons away at all costs.

Let's read Galatians 5:22-23 and list the characteristics of the Holy Spirit that are produced in us as Christ followers:

love, joy, peace, patience, kindness, goodness, faithfulness, gentleness & self-control

See a familiar word in there?

When my oldest niece was two, a popular sentence in her vocabulary was "Gotta be patient. Gotta wait." I asked her if she was excited for Christmas, and she replied, "Gotta be patient. Gotta wait." Another time I asked her if she was excited for a play date, and she simply answered, "Gotta be patient. Gotta wait." Even her answer about if she was ready for dinner was met with her cute little voice, "Godda be pashent. Godda wait." You get the point. The message of patience is easy for her to understand—she has something to look forward to, but the time isn't now. She trusts the words her parents have told her, and as a result, doesn't doubt that Christmas morning will come, the doorbell will ring, and dinner will be put on the table.

I want that kind of patience. I want to trust my Father enough where those words roll off my tongue, "Gotta be patient. Gotta wait." I want to tell you I am fully embracing every aspect of our wait, but truthfully, some days are harder than others. Impatience never seems to result in positive attitudes or joyful hearts. Those kinds of days are typically the ones seasoned with a bad attitude and irritation (mostly self-inflicted).

Hebrews 12 talks about running "with endurance the race that is set before us." What comfort my heart takes in knowing that God has a path placed before me! We are not the ones making the way and paving the path. Instead, we are called to meet Him at the starting line, to roll up our sleeves, and to charge ahead.

In these times when patience is tested and the answers seem to be out of sight, God whispers, "*I will be everything you need in these moments of waiting.*" So instead of asking, "God, are we there yet?" which only seems to breed impatience, let's ask, "God, what are You trying to teach me?" Once we start reflecting on the lessons to be learned, it makes the wait feel worth it, and our joy becomes more abundant.

live deeper

James 1:12 teaches us about how God rewards patience. Jot down the blessing God provides to those who patiently endure testing and temptation.

great blessings

Our patience does pay off! Read through Psalm 40:1-3 and reflect below how this verse comforts you in your wait today.

reflection

I love how *The Message* translates Colossians 1:11-12. As you read through it, circle the words or phrases that stand out to you.

> We pray that you'll have the strength to stick it out over the long haul—not the grim strength of gritting your teeth but the glory strength God gives. It is strength that endures the unendurable and spills over into joy, thanking the Father who makes us strong enough to take part in everything bright and beautiful that He has for us.

I find that when I allow my impatience to run wild, my joy plummets. Pause and reflect back over the past few days. How have you seen impatience have a negative effect on your joy?

How can we actively choose to wait patiently when we don't know future plans?

To trust and continue to cherish the current situation

What is God teaching you about patience in this season of wait?

To believe that he knows your heart desire

recognizing blessings

Don't worry about anything; instead, pray about everything.
Tell God what you need, and thank him for all he has
done. Then you will experience God's peace, which exceeds
anything we can understand. His peace will guard your
hearts and minds as you live in Christ Jesus.
PHILLIPPIANS 4:6-7 (NLT)

A few years ago the only thing I could see was the giant
puzzle piece that was missing from our life: a baby. I prayed,
oh, I prayed so hard. I prayed through the worry. I prayed
for what I needed. I prayed for what we wanted. But I felt
unfulfilled; the peace just wasn't quite there, and neither was
our baby.

And then I read—*really read*—the passage from
Philippians and saw the sentence that has completely

changed my life, completely changed my joy: "...*and thank Him for all He has done* (4:6 (NLT), emphasis mine).

In 2012, my word of the year became "gratitude." I was determined to focus on becoming a woman who doesn't just pray through my list, but instead, prays with a grateful heart. I needed some motivation. I decided in order to be intentional about it, accountability was needed. I started a Facebook album entitled {2012 - PhotoAday - thankful}. By the end of every day, I reflected and uploaded a photo that described something I was thankful for that day. Now it may sound easy, but there were days when everything went wrong and it was hard. It was hard to see past the argument I had with my husband, the climbing automotive bill, or the miscarriage on Christmas day. My eyes wanted to focus on the bad, the miserable, the frustrations, but I didn't allow myself to go there because I had to find that one moment, luxury, or gift that brought joy to my day.

I did this for 731 straight days. Some days it was big things like a fun outing with my family or laughing with girlfriends. Other days it was the scent of a Macintosh apple candle or tissues with lotion after a day filled with tears.

I began to learn to see the big and small moments that filled my heart with thanksgiving. I've by no means perfected it, but I no longer need the accountability.

It seems silly that something as trivial as a Facebook album could change my heart and prayer life, but it did. It started by changing my attitude and my words to Him. It removed the temptation to focus solely on myself, what I needed, and what I was lacking. It lifted my eyes off of myself and to the blessings I have been given.

Think about it: Every day we wake up. We get dressed and put on clean clothes, (assuming we did the laundry, most likely in a washer and dryer). We can go to the refrigerator, which holds food to feed our families, at least enough to get through the day. We sip fancy coffee from coffee shops, have friends that make us laugh, peruse social media on our handheld devices, and have the ability to open up a Bible at any time. Compared to some, our lives, as tough as they feel some days, are hardly that.

Write out Psalm 118:24 below. (I love the NLT version!)

A grateful heart recognizes just how many blessings we are given, even when the hard parts are big and painful and overwhelming. Seasons of waiting and hardships are the devil's playground for creating bitterness. There seems to be a magnetic force that causes our eyes to notice what we are lacking. Do you want a child? *Look at all these people who have a baby but you!* Are you waiting for Mr. Right to come along? *You're the only one who's still single!* Do you want a new car? *Nobody else has rust on theirs!*

Lacking. Missing. Unfulfilled. The devil loves to spotlight our areas of longing. And then we become bitter. Angry. Resentful.

A great way to destroy the temptation to wallow is to intentionally notice all we have been given. It can be difficult on a daily basis but the good news is we don't need to pursue a grateful heart on our own. God promises to come alongside of us to transform our hearts.

One of my pastors, Jason Strand, once said, "So many of us are looking for a change to our circumstances when what we really need is a change in our perspective." *Wham!* I love the reminder that our circumstances are merely that, circumstantial situations. It's how we view our lives that really makes the difference.

Let's take our eyes off of ourselves, start counting our blessings, and rejoice in the fact that we are abundantly cared for. We can become women who are filled with unspeakable joy, and as we rejoice, the silver lining will become easier for us to see.

dive deeper

1 Thessalonians 5:16-18 hits hard when it talks about joy and circumstances. In light of this verse, what do you take away?

Psalm 28:7 (GW) shares a way we can give thanks. What is it? What way do you best praise Him?

How can you become a person of intentional gratitude today? What could that look like for you? For example, creating gratitude lists, singing worship songs, writing out scripture, or sharing with a friend. Don't let today slip away without thinking about this. Then do more than just think—begin!

reflection

Pause and think about the season that's most weighing on your heart right now. The desire that keeps you up at night or causes your soul weariness. Now take some time to think about the good things that have come as a result.

Lord, thank you for who You are and the gifts that I have been given. Thank you for Your mercy, grace, and love. My heart desires to become a person who recognizes the blessings in the chaos. I pray that You guide me as I strive to become a person who is always joyful, thanking You despite the circumstances. Open my eyes to the blessings all around me. Amen.

being filled with hope

Rejoice in our confident hope. Be patient
in trouble, and keep on praying.
ROMANS 12:12 (NLT)

"Stay hopeful!" is a phrase that's often thrown at me. It's a universal statement to never give up, keep trying, and to remain positive. It sounds good, but it can be so draining to remain optimistic. How do we remain hopeful when our souls are brittle and weary?

Take a minute to look up Hebrews 10:23 (NLT). What does it teach us about hope?

To hold on to the hope we have, never hesitating to tell people about it. We can trust god to do what he promised

Our hope is not rooted in answered prayers, in the possibility of brighter days, or the struggles of life to be over. Our hope is rooted in God, our True Hope. He is faithful. He has overcome everything. That's it, bottom line, God wins!

Our verse today from Romans talks about rejoicing in our "confident hope". Miriam Webster tells us confident means "firmly trusting and believing, having strong certainty of and being fully assured." Let me be transparent with you: I don't know that my hope in God is always fully-assured. I battle with having a power struggle over wanting the control and then giving it back to Him.

When we are exhausted, hope seems hard to attain. It's in these moments we have to make a choice. The first option is to change where we direct our hope, investing it into a new medical treatment, business plan, or dating website. We can displace where hope is rooted and try to change the outcome to something we can control a bit more. Sometimes this option seems to go well until it fails and disappoints, which it inevitably will. Our hope cannot be rooted in things!

The second option is this: we press into God. We march forward with determination, and believe with faith that He is trustworthy. We begin to build our relationship with God, getting to know Him more intimately, becoming tender to His voice. We then begin to allow ourselves to be led by Him. You know what I have found to be true? He meets us and doesn't let us down, even when things don't go the way we anticipate.

God is not early or late with His timing. Instead, He is right on cue, creating "Ah-ha!" moments when the answered prayers finally come. Yes, it may look different than we expect it to, but, we know He will pull through. Scripture reminds us that we can trust Him to stay true to His Word, character, and promises. *His love is always present.* Breathe out a deep sigh with me today and rest assured knowing He is at work, even when we don't see it.

Shauna Niequist says, "Just because I have forgotten how to see doesn't mean it isn't there. His goodness is there. His promises have been kept. All I need to do is see." How can we open our eyes today to notice Him?

Hope is much deeper than an emotion; it believes He has plans for this season. It is our foundation.

What does God say to the Israelites in Jeremiah 29:11-13? How can truly believing this deepen your hope in Him?

We have hope because we have a God who loves us personally, intimately, and wants the best for us. We have hope because even when we don't understand, He does.

When we live with God at the center and our hope is rooted in Him, something powerful and beautiful happens. It transforms our hearts to believe, *truly believe,* that God knows better than we do. That He can be trusted. He has been faithful in the past and His faithfulness will only continue. Our lives are woven with His goodness. So, let us *"hold tightly without wavering to the hope we affirm, for God can be trusted to keep his promises"* (Hebrews 10:23 (NLT), emphasis mine).

dive deeper

The word "hope" goes far beyond our wish list. Take the time to look up these verses and write down a summary of what each one tells us about our hope.

Psalm 33:20-22

Psalm 39:7

Psalm 119:114, 116

Romans 15:13

Hebrews 11:1

reflection

Shauna Niequist writes, "Hope always feels impossible before we commit to it." Reflect on what this means in your life.

Memorization can be hard, but the Word shows it's needed for many reasons (Deuteronomy 6:4-9; Joshua 1:8; Psalm 119:9, 11; Matthew 4; Ephesians 6:10-20).

Go back to the verses in the *Dive Deeper* section, and choose one to memorize. Write it down and place it somewhere you'll see it regularly. You can use your phone to record your voice and listen to it throughout your day.

In the space below, select your verse and write it out, identifying what you will do to help you memorize it.

Lord, thank you for the hope that You give to me. I ask You to help me commit to believing You are trustworthy and that Your plans for my future are good. Strengthen me to rest assured knowing You're faithful always. Amen.

finding joy in the wait

Dear brothers and sisters, when troubles of any kind come your way, consider it an opportunity for great joy.
JAMES 1:2 (NLT)

Can you believe we have made it to the end of week four? All we've talked about—overcoming guilt, surviving tested faith, practicing patience, recognizing our blessings, and being filled with hope—play into the true joy we experience as believers. Joy that is rooted in Him, not on our circumstances. Joy that comes as a result of the trials we face even though they are difficult.

Take a moment to reread James 1:2. How does this verse apply to what God has taught you this week?

What did you learn this week?
What was your biggest take away?

Challenge: take what you've learned one step further. Write a note to yourself with your above thoughts. Seal it up in a preaddressed envelope with a stamp and give it to a trusted friend, asking them to mail it to you in 6 months. What a blessing it will be to read how God has moved in your heart several months from now!

victory in the wait

Victory. In a season of waiting, where sorrow, pain, and unmet expectations are aplenty, that word can seem far off. Improbable. Unattainable. Maybe even a bad joke.

But as Christ followers, that's exactly what our Lord promises us: Victory. He speaks success and triumph over our enemy. And in our battle and war, He claims we have everything we need to come out the other end; our soul unscathed, untouched, pure as gold.

Pit that against our waiting circumstances, and there can be quite the disparity. Job loss, infertility, loneliness. Bankruptcy, a rebellious child, a move across borders and away from family. For me, I was diagnosed with Hodgkin's Lymphoma 3 years ago and thought I was clear out of the woods health-wise. But as of late, my feet have been tingling. Combine that with blurred vision, headaches, dizziness, and muscle spasms, and the neurologist is testing me for MS and the like.

The pressures of this world can indeed be mounting and the fear suffocating, but again and even still, even in the grim when our knees are shaking, we are still told the victory is ours.

How? On what grounds? Sunday school answer: Jesus.

prepare your heart for the week

Where have you seen God's victory after a waiting season in your life? What do you hope to learn this week in the arena of victory?

claiming victory

For we do not have a high priest who is unable to empathize
with our weaknesses, but we have one
who has been tempted in every way,
just as we are - yet he did not sin.

HEBREWS 4:15

Why do some days fly, but others drag along, slow as a
turtle, the unhurried tick of the clock the most annoying
sound known to man? My next doctor appointment isn't for
another week, and the wait engulfs me; the tingling is my
constant reminder. I keep going back to the moment when
the doctor first told me I had cancer, and it's easy to imagine
bad news once again. But I'm called to hope. Even more so,
hope with confidence.

I keep asking myself... *how?*

Jesus is our example for all things: He's the Perfecter of our faith, the unblemished Man, our holy God, and our High Priest, who constantly lives to intercede for us. To Him, we can look to for wisdom, as the model for victorious living, and through Him, we can find the answer to that question of how.

Read Matthew 4:1-11. When Jesus was led into the wilderness for a 40-day battle with the serpent, He was attacked from every angle. Trying to nail His hunger, the enemy tempted Him with the idea of loaves of bread. Hoping to get under His skin, the devil poked at His divinity—if You're the Son of God, prove it; make God save You. And his last-ditch effort was to fuel pride; if You bow to me, I will give You kingship over the entire world.

Where do you find yourself most vulnerable? If you were in the battle with the serpent, what angle would he attack? Would he go for your pride or ego? Possibly your insecurities riddled with past mistakes? A doubt or fear you carry close? Or would he attack a desire that you repeatedly just can't restrain?

Regardless what it is, notice how Jesus responds in every case and against every attack. Each time the enemy ran his mouth, Jesus declared a stronger word. He, who was fully God and fully Man, fought against every temptation by claiming truth and a verse in Scripture, always beginning with, "It is written." Jesus knew who He was, and He proclaimed it in relation to God's Word.

Do you know who you are? Not just your height, weight, and occupation. But do you really know who you are—in relation to God's Word? Who does God say you are? Take a minute to write down how you'd describe your identity—feel free to use adjectives, titles, or pictures!

Let me throw out a few to add to your list. You are a child of God, chosen, armed with strength, and more than a conqueror. Together, we are a holy people, the salt of the world, a royal priesthood, a brotherhood of believers. The called, the elect, the sons of light, and His witnesses. We are healed, redeemed, righteous, and pure. We are strong, and through the power of Christ, we are *victorious*.

You know what I find interesting? Flip back a page in your Bible to the previous chapter: Matthew 3:13-17. The event that took place right before Jesus was led into the wilderness was His own baptism. There He took a giant step forward in His obedience to the Father, and in turn, God opened up the heavens and sent His Spirit down like a dove to rest on Jesus. And loudly, for everyone to hear, the voice from heaven declared, "This is my dearly loved Son, who brings me great joy" (Matthew 3:17 (NLT)).

Jesus was told by God Himself who He was: *His dearly loved Son*. Yet, the very next place Jesus finds Himself in is the desert being tempted by Satan. Seems foolish of the enemy to tempt Jesus when He was *just* lathered up with truth and affirmation and God's Spirit.

God wants this same position for us. If we stock up in the truth of our identity, yes, it would be foolish for Satan to attack us *just* when we've built up our confidence. But that's the point. That's our example. That's how we find our victory.

Today, when the battle is bloody and the waiting is hard and the enemy is sounding off, stake your claim. Start with, "It is written." And speak a stronger word. Boast in the name of the Lord and in the names He's given you because when you do, God promises "we will rise up and stand firm" (Psalm 20:7-8 (NLT)). And ultimately, with Him at your right hand, you will not be shaken (Psalm 16:8 (NLT)).

dive deeper

After reading Matthew 4:1-11, what key words or phrases stuck out to you?

Read Hebrews 4:15-16. What areas in your life have you been recently tempted? What needs, desires, and hopes do you cherish most? How can we view Jesus in light of our weaknesses?

Out of all the names God has given us, which is most meaningful to you? How can you remember this name as part of your identity today?

reflection

Jesus fought back against the enemy with Scripture because
He knew it like the back of His hand. We've learned that
memorizing Scripture can serve as a powerful reminder, so
choose one verse today and splash it across your lock screen,
write it on your bathroom mirror, or create a melody that's
easy to hum. Whatever it takes, keep it on the forefront of
your mind throughout the day.

Dear Jesus, I love that You were both fully God and fully
human as You walked this earth. Because that means You
understand me—my weaknesses, my temptations, and my
doubts! I thank you for Your example of victory—by claiming
a better word through "it is written." I pray that You would
equip me to fight my own battles through my chosen verse
today as I'm wandering in my own wilderness. I thank you
for Your presence and strength. Amen.

experiencing opposition

We demolish arguments and every pretension that sets itself up against the knowledge of God, and we take captive every thought to make it obedient to Christ.

2 CORINTHIANS 10:5

All throughout the Old Testament, the Israelites had a hard time accepting God's plan to save them. *What if our enemies are stronger? What if we starve? Even worse, what if we die out here in the wilderness?*

But if we are being honest with ourselves, how often do we sound like the Israelites in our own lives? *What if I lose my job? How will I be able to pay my mortgage? Even worse, how could I afford Starbucks?!*

Yes, there's definitely a real enemy out there, and he doesn't carry the best intentions. Read John 10:10. Jesus is clear with us: Satan comes to steal and kill and destroy, and it's important to recognize that. But as evil as he is, and as easy as it would be to blame every mishap, error, and pain on his devilish schemes, it isn't too far-fetched that we carry part of the blame.

Isn't it so easy to work against ourselves? We allow our minds to drag us down a dozen bunny trails until we've reached every worst-case scenario. Like for me, just in the past hour, I've logged onto WebMD and wavered between a self-diagnosis of ALS, MS, Parkinson's, and a panic disorder. I didn't even notice stiff muscles before, but after reading the symptoms—now that I think about it—some areas do seem tight! And just like that, after a few short clicks and some reading, I was a hot mess. Another week of this while waiting for the results? Torture.

Our thoughts can be so toxic in the wait, can't they? Sometimes they can seem silly when you say them out loud or after a full night's rest. But in the moment, friends, we cannot let our minds run rampant! We've got to rein it in! When we allow those destructive thoughts to take over our emotions and dictate our actions, that's exactly what happens: we destruct. We poison our lot, and we hand over our victory.

So we must fight back. We've got to do whatever it takes to regain control and heed to the warning God gave the Israelites. All throughout Exodus, Numbers, and Deuteronomy, God delivered His people from slavery, parted the Red Sea for their escape, gave them food falling daily from the sky, and promised to lead the way with a cloud in the day and fire by night.

Yet, they still went down those bunny trails. They whispered to one another and soon bemoaned loudly to God: *Why have You led us out here? When will we get there? We used to eat as much fish as we wanted in Egypt, but here? All we have is manna!*

Seems incredulous, even ridiculous on this side, doesn't it? God had so obviously saved them from slavery. He provided in miraculous ways where food literally fell from the sky every day. Yet they still questioned Him? Still doubted His intentions? Still couldn't see His goodness? All God needed from them was faith. To trust Him, His plans, and His power. But their wayward thoughts wouldn't let that happen.

What are the what-if's in your life? *What if we never get pregnant? What if we never get out of debt? What if I never lose this weight? What if I stay single forever?* Take time to call it out, and write them down.

When our minds start rambling down this road, this is where we need to watch out; this is the dangerous territory. Because these bunny trails and toxic thoughts may lead us astray from the victory God has for us; exactly like what happened with the Israelites.

Unfortunately, their fear and doubt kept them from entering the Promised Land. God made it very clear that because of this disbelief, they wouldn't step foot in this land overflowing with milk and honey, except for two fine young men who kept the faith. Ever heard of Joshua and Caleb? Until tomorrow, friends.

Today, we've got to learn from the Israelites and rein it in and take every thought captive to the obedience of Christ.

Read 2 Corinthians 10:5. How has God saved you? When has He been faithful in the past? How has He provided for you? Make a list, because these are the moments we need to focus on. When our thoughts begin to spiral out of control, all God asks is that we choose faith. To trust Him, His plans, and His power. Don't forget the things He's done for you, and take heart in knowing that He is not holding out on you and is not done with you yet!

In the words of Steven Furtick: "The voice you believe will determine the future you experience." What future do you hope for? What thoughts line up with that future? What voice have you been listening to, and if it's not God's voice, how can you instead tune into Him above all else?

Read Ephesians 6:10-18. As we recognize and know there is opposition, how can you be strong in the Lord and in His mighty power? What piece of armor do you need to intentionally put on today?

reflection

Seems unbelievable that the Israelites would ever doubt God after all the miracles He performed right in front of their eyes. Yet, to them, their doubts were valid. In your wait, what fears may you be experiencing that appear legitimate? How may you need to choose faith instead today?

Dear Lord, I honestly want to trust You. I know that You and Your plans are good, but sometimes, I have a hard time swallowing that and seeing past my hurt and fear. It's hard to believe anything good will come out of this season of waiting...but today, I choose faith. When it's easy to doubt, I refuse. I want to enter the Promised Land You have for me, so please give me the grace and strength today to be faithful to You. In Jesus' powerful name, I pray. Amen.

knowing the truth

"For I know the plans I have for you," says the Lord.
"They are plans for good and not for disaster,
to give you a future and a hope."
JEREMIAH 29:11

Do you know God has a purpose for your life? He didn't just create you to breathe in oxygen, exhale carbon dioxide, and take up space. And He didn't send you into this world merely to survive it.

God created you, forming your inward being, sculpting a plan for your life, and instilling a personality, sense of direction, and a calling into your soul. And He arms you with strength, victory, and a plan, so that every day can be purposeful!

Just the same, God had a plan for the Israelites. They wandered throughout the wilderness, yes, and at times felt like their suffering was unbearable wondering if the Promised Land would ever come. But God kept reminding His people that He was up to something. That He was taking care of them. That if they would only hold on, His good plans would come to pass and they would settle in a land overflowing with milk and honey.

Have there been times when the waiting seemed heavy-handed? When you wondered how long you'd have to stay in the wilderness? So much so you almost lost hope in a good future?

What's *your* Promised Land? Where do you hope to be after this season of waiting? If everything went according to plan, where's the ultimate destination?

I have recurring oncology appointments every 6 months to be sure my body is rid of cancer, and on top of that, I've had MRIs to check for MS and mole removals to test for melanoma. It constantly feels like I never get a break from the doctor, and as I hold my breath every time waiting on the results, it's hard to see the purpose. I so badly long for a break hoping for a healthy future to grow old with my husband and see my kids grow up.

In all of this though, I've come to find it's much easier to walk by sight, and not by faith. Like once I get a good health report, then I can have confidence again in my body. Or maybe once I stop feeling the tingling in my feet, then I can move onto a good future. It's easy to be short-sighted like this and think purely in the short-term, because anything beyond the now is unclear.

But it's in this uncharted territory that God calls us to live the opposite: by faith, not by sight. To not let the physical reminders and current circumstances sway our thinking, because when has God ever needed all the odds stacked in His favor anyway? There's no need for us to focus on the horizontal, our present circumstances, because we're called to set our eyes above, fixating vertically on who God is.

It's here, when we understand and know the character of God—that He is trustworthy, faithful, and true; the God of the impossible—then, we have reason for hope regardless of our positive or negative circumstances. Because through the sacrifice of Jesus Christ, we can trust that God has a purpose for our lives, He will carry it to completion (Philippians 1:6), and He will work all things for our good (Romans 8:28).

God did eventually lead His people out of their wilderness and into the Promised Land. But like we talked about yesterday, it wasn't the original group of Israelites that He saved from slavery; it happened to be the next generation that experienced this gift. I think it's important to remember why again: because their fathers and mothers let fear and their own plans get in the way. They just couldn't figure out how to trust in God's mysterious ways so they forfeited the land God had prepared for them.

But Joshua and Caleb stayed resilient in faith, and because they were strong and courageous enough to believe God's plans were better than their own, they were escorted into the Promised Land.

Today, we are given the same ultimatum. In our waiting, throughout the trials and in all the unknown, we can either respond like the former Israelites and give into doubt and stay firm in our own plans. Or, like Joshua and Caleb, we can relinquish control over our present day, and choose to stay resilient, remembering God's plans *are* good and remaining strong in faith. The choice is there and how we answer will pave the way of our future. Will we remain in the wilderness, or will we step foot into our Promised Land?

Let's be the Joshua's and Caleb's of our day, and choose unwavering faith! Let's refuse to be bogged down by the what-if's, because we know our God is stronger than any worst-case scenario. And let's hold on in our season of waiting, entrusting our future to the God who has a good plan for our lives doing whatever it takes to walk by faith *regardless* of what's in sight.

dive deeper

Read Jeremiah 29:10-14. What good things has God promised in your life? What are God's intentions for you and your future? How can you find God in your season of waiting?

What are your plans, goals, and aspirations? In a perfect world, how do you envision your future in one year? Five years? Ten years? How can you align your plans with God's plans?

Read Isaiah 55:8-9. Why are our visions sometimes different than God's? When our plans fail or the direction changes, why might that be? Why can we trust God?

reflection

What may possibly be God's plan for your life? How have you seen Him move you toward a certain mission, call, or pounding heartbeat? How has God reminded you in this season of waiting that He is still up to something? What do you need to do to continue holding on for your Promised Land?

I ather, thank you for Your sovereign ways. You are good, and Your plans for me are equally as good. You don't want me to see disaster, but rather, You want me to prosper. When I look toward my future, You want me to see hope. And for that, I couldn't be more grateful. Teach me how to live like Joshua and Caleb with open hands and a relentless faith, and continue to guide me along the path to my Promised I and. I trust You above all else.

In Jesus' name, I pray. Amen.

your promised land

> *The Lord commanded us to obey all these decrees and to
> fear the Lord our God, so that we might always prosper
> and be kept alive, as is the case today.*
> DEUTERONOMY 6:24

Let's hone in on our man Joshua. His faith? Unwavering, uncontested. And the four principles we can gain from Joshua 3 alone can help us move forward in our own waiting to the victory and Promised Land we so desire.

Read Joshua 3:1-5. Before Joshua led the Israelites across the Jordan, he gave them a bold promise of hope: "Purify yourselves, for tomorrow the Lord will do great wonders among you" (NLT, vs. 5).

<u>Principle 1: Have hope for tomorrow.</u> You may be waiting today, not getting what you want now, and unsure how the tables could ever turn. But with God, *all* things really are possible, and anything can turn on a dime. As we wait, we need to take heart and know that God will use our tomorrow in mighty ways if we keep the faith.

Read Joshua 3:6-10. Joshua told the people over and over again: God is on our side. Sure, they would face the Canaanites, Hittites, Hivites, Perizzites, Girgashites, Amorites, and Jebusites (now that's a mouthful!). All powerful, fear-evoking enemies. But God was living among them, and He promised to drive them out. There was simply no reason to believe otherwise!

<u>Principle 2: God is living among us, and He is on our side.</u> We need to let that truth marinate deep down in our spirits—especially when we look to the left and to the right, only seeing trouble, defeat, and dead ends. Because, like the Israelites, we are given the promise of victory, and we simply have no reason to believe otherwise.

Read Joshua 3:12-15. He then passed along God's command to the priests carrying the Ark of the Covenant: "When you reach the bank of the Jordan River, take a few steps into the river and stop there. As soon as their feet touch the water, the flow of the water will be cut off upstream, and the river will stand up like a wall" (NLT, vs. 8, 13).

<u>Principle 3: We need to keep going.</u> It would be the easy way out to curl up in bed, pull the covers over our head, and wait safely in our pajamas until circumstances change. But that's not exactly how God works; what kind of life would

that be anyway? Instead, He wants us to *persevere*. Because when we move forward in faith and get ankle-deep in the water, that's when God parts our Jordan. Then we can claim victory and get to our Promised Land.

Read Joshua 3:16-17. With Joshua's order, the people left their camp to cross the Jordan. Even though the river's banks were overflowing thanks to harvest season, the priests moved ahead in faith and waited in the middle of the riverbed until the whole nation of Israel crossed the Jordan on dry ground.

Principle 4: The Lord's hand is powerful. He has the ability to do anything and everything. He could have stopped the waters well before His people left their campsite, so the passage would be ready for them to walk through when they got there. But God wanted their faith. You can bet their eyes popped out as they witnessed the waves crashing and the banks flooding, but even still, they listened to their God. And once they were ankle-deep in the water, they saw the Lord's hand move in a miraculous way—a miracle they may have missed altogether if they stayed put in their campsite waiting like bumps on a log. Even when science screams otherwise, the Israelites crossed on dry ground because they served the God who controls all things.

Some days, I spring out of bed with a can-do attitude and a surrendering faith to Jesus. I don't even care what lies ahead because I know the God who is already there and I know He will take care of me. But other days, it's hard for me to peel my eyes off the weird looking mole or take my mind off the twitch in my neck. It's those days that I'm staring down at the treacherous river instead of lifting up my chin to the God who controls those waters.

I don't know what river you're staring at today, but together, let's live out the four principles from Joshua 3: have hope for tomorrow, know that God is on our side, keep going, and recognize above all that the Lord's hand is powerful. When we do, we can trust God *will* make a way for us to move forward onto dry ground.

dive deeper

What river are you staring at these days? Are the waters raging and the banks intimidating? Read Psalm 18:35. What has God given you to use in these types of situations?

Have you been waiting for a sign or an opportunity like the
Israelites at their campsite? Or have you been actively
seeking God and getting ankle-deep in your circumstances?
Describe where you see yourself: in the campsite, on the
water's edge, in the water, or walking across dry land.

Read Zephaniah 3:17 in the NIV. When the Mighty Warrior
is living among you, who could be against you?

reflection

How can you take one step further in the waters today?

Lord, I praise You for Your powerful hand, and how You extend that same power and victory to me. I want to keep going in my wait and present circumstances, because I choose to have hope in tomorrow. I choose to have faith in Your ways. Help me to take another step to get ankle deep in the water, and show me Your faithfulness as You part the flood and river before me. Amen.

victory in your story

They triumphed over him by the blood of the Lamb and by the word of their testimony...
REVELATION 12:11

Whenever I swing back to fear, lamenting my tingling legs, bewailing about all my health scares, and throwing out the ever famous "Why me?!" my husband is quick to declare truth and doesn't let me get by or move on until I've also declared the same out loud.

"You're right... God's Word tells me I am healed. My times are in His hands. He will go before me. He will never leave me. If God is on my side, who can be against me?" And the more I claim these nuggets of Scripture, the less fear I feel, and the further it gives way to true confidence. I almost start to say this thread of truth even with a bit of anger, like how dare anyone or anything ever convince me otherwise!

Because it's true, our words carry tremendous influence and power. They can tear us down, or they can build us up. They can breathe out hope and praise the one true God, or they can be filled with anger and curse His ways.

Reminisce about a time when your words carried such influence.

God Himself shows the power behind words. Think about creation. He simply spoke it to be; He didn't wave His arms around like a magician or do some sort of ceremonial dance. God said let there be, and there was. In the same way, when Jesus' disciples were scared of the storm rocking their boat, all Jesus had to say was, "Silence! Be still!" and the winds stopped and the waves calmed (Mark 4:39 (NLT)). And yet, Jesus left this world saying we'll do even greater works than He Himself did (John 14:12). Greater than stopping thunder by three words?! As unbelievable as it may seem, Jesus thought so.

So what kind of words are you saying? Utilizing? Declaring? Because ultimately, when it comes to victory, what you say carries all the power: "And they have defeated [the accuser] by the blood of the Lamb and by their testimony" (Revelations 12:11 (NLT)).

You have a story to share, a testimony of God's victory in your life. But are you sharing it? Are you telling others of the great works God has done in your life? Words filled with hope and meaning and triumph? Or are your stories shadowed with fear and resignation? Words that point to you and away from the glory of God?

The enemy doesn't want beauty or truth to come from our story. Like attacking Jesus in the wilderness, he wants to hit us from every angle and force us into the shadows, away from a platform of influence.

Don't let him.

You are the light of this world, a city on a hill. Because of the Holy Spirit living inside of you, you are a force to be reckoned with, so let it shine, let it shine, let it shine.

I instinctively like to keep my cards close to my chest when it comes to health issues. I cringe at the pity, the thought of being less than, and really would like to avoid the "did you hear what happened?" gossip trains. Plus, my medical file is pretty thick already, so at this point, anything additional just seems like I'm making stuff up.

But the blog posts where I'm most transparent receive the most engagement. And the conversations when I lay it all out on the table? Those who sit across from me open up in ways that just leave me blinking hard. Because authenticity is valued, and when you share your story, it gives people a chance to say, "Me too!" It opens their eyes to things otherwise unseen.

Today, refuse to believe the lie that your story is less than. So you fell into awful habits of drugs and were addicted to the bottle? Your testimony shows how God removes sin as far as the east is from the west. You grew up in a Christian home without anything catastrophic or obvious waywardness? Your story shows the beauty of God's grace protecting and enveloping you at such an early age.

Point is: your story matters. You have something to say, and God wants you to say it. You reveal an aspect of His character and a portion of God's personality like no one else can do. You are an important piece to the puzzle of the body of Christ.

Let's not let the enemy gain any more ground by being silent; it's time to claim back some of that victory. Remember, you carry the power. Whatever you do today, find a way to tell someone how Jesus has impacted you, and watch the victory of God seep into your conversations, your life, and your story.

Read James 3:2-10. How is your tongue and the words you speak impactful? What's the potential and what's the curse?

Read Matthew 5:14-16. How can you give light to everyone in the house through your story?

Read 2 Corinthians 1:3-7. If you are like me and like to keep private things private, how can you challenge yourself to open up and share your troubles with those around you? What may God want to use in your life to help you comfort others?

reflection

What is your story? Summarize in 1-3 bullet points.

-

-

-

How can you share your story? What are those trigger conversations for you? For me, when someone asks about my health or any updates on testing, that's my trigger. I don't just share the facts; I transparently communicate how God was in it, gave me peace, and answered my prayers. When we give glory to Him by the word of our testimony, we overcome.

Jesus, I want to share more of my story, so people hear more of Your story. Give me boldness to speak and opportunities to tell my story, and teach me how to be intentional with my words. I look to You for confidence and victory, and through the testimony You have given me, I know I can overcome. Thank you for the unique way You're working in my life! In Jesus' powerful name, I pray. Amen.

finding victory in the wait

In the past month, I've been to the doctor and neurologist, sat through a couple MRI's and x-rays, and given blood for labs to check my organs and vitamin levels. After each appointment and test, there was waiting. P-L-E-N-T-Y of waiting. Days when my mind escaped down the bunny trail of what-if's, and days when I stood ankle deep in the water claiming victory.

And that's life. Because we're humans. We aren't perfect, and try as we may, our faith isn't perfect either. That's why we need Jesus, the Author and Perfecter of our faith. He will take hold of our right hand and carry us when the days are hard, and He will stand with us in our joy when the days are easy. But regardless of which side of the pendulum we're swinging toward today, Jesus is there, and He is true; and ultimately, HE is the victory. Knowing Him, growing in relationship with Him, and learning from Him is what it's all about.

What's something new that you learned this week? What was a good reminder? What is your biggest takeaway?

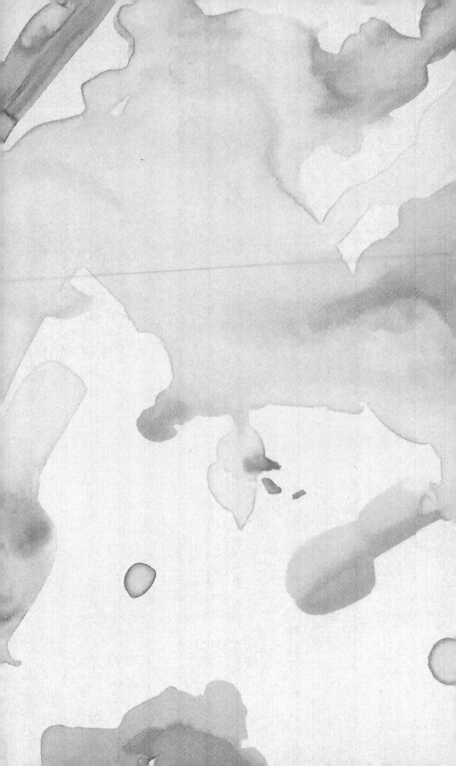

gratitude in the wait

The simple act of gratitude has the power to transform our lives from one of defeat into one of true joy. Countless times we find ourselves looking at the glass that seems to be half empty, forgetting there is still life-giving water inside. When we give thanks, we find we actually have more than enough!

Throughout Scripture, we see others giving thanks for the circumstances right in front of them. David gives thanks repeatedly throughout the Psalms. Jesus gives thanks for the five loaves and two fish which multiplied to feed the five thousand (Matthew 14:19-21) and even before His death (Luke 22:19). We also see Paul giving thanks in all situations he faced, from imprisonments to shipwrecks and more (1 Thessalonians 5:18). Many more examples could be listed!

This week, all five of us are coming together with you to dive into gratitude. Giving thanks slows us down and opens our eyes to the blessings all around. We can learn to give thanks—no matter what.

prepare your heart for the week

Identify the areas in your life in which you struggle with gratitude. What do you hope to learn by diving into thankfulness this week?

green pastures

*Then we your people, the sheep of your pasture, will thank
you forever and ever, praising your greatness from
generation to generation.*
PSALM 79:13 (NLT)

I love when God answers prayers quickly, don't you?
My friend and I prayed together one evening and we asked
the Lord to encourage my heart. Nothing in my life was
falling apart, but I needed my spirit to be renewed and my
heart encouraged.

As we prayed, a hymn popped into her head: *Be Still
My Soul.* We looked up the words, and the first two stanzas
go like this:

Be still, my soul; the Lord is on thy side;
Bear patiently the cross of grief or pain;
Leave to thy God to order and provide;
In every change He faithful will remain.
Be still, my soul; thy best, thy heavenly, Friend
Through thorny ways leads to a joyful end.

Be still, my soul; thy God doth undertake
To guide the future as He has the past.
Thy hope, thy confidence, let nothing shake;
All now mysterious shall be bright at last.
Be still, my soul; the waves and winds still know
His voice who ruled them while He dwelt below.

It amazed me how some of these words uplifted me right on the spot! But what I couldn't even imagine was, as the weeks went by, each line, and soon *the whole hymn*, spoke directly into my circumstances.

As I see how God led me during this time, I can't help but think of Psalm 23. This psalm is well known because of the comforting imagery. It describes Jesus as our Shepherd; us as a bunch of little lambs.

Read Psalm 23:1-4 and write verse 1 below.

In each waiting season, there may be bright days and dark nights. Are we letting God refresh our souls when we are in "green pastures"? So often, when it's smooth sailing, it's easy to get caught up in the blue skies and lose sight of our Shepherd! Even if things seem to be going well, I urge you, still seek Him! He has us in the green pasture for a reason—and He wants to strengthen us for valleys up ahead.

As my friend and I prayed together, the circumstances in my life were equivalent to a windy day. I didn't *have* to ask the Lord to encourage me. I could have made it through. But, I think back to that day, and I am so thankful I drew close to Jesus.

Jesus knows something we don't. Even when life is going well, it's inevitable: a valley may be around the corner. As I meditated on the words my Shepherd led me to, He was refreshing my soul. And not only refreshed my soul for that day, but also prepared my soul for what was up ahead! And I know the same is true for you.

Depending on God during every aspect of our waiting season gives us a glimpse into who God is.

Will you do something with me today? Let's recognize ourselves as God's sheep. Let's give thanks to God—and let's declare His goodness to those around us—because He is the best Shepherd we could ever ask for! He strengthens us today because He knows what tomorrow holds. Let's cling to Him, not only when the going gets tough, but also when the blue skies are all around!

dive deeper

Read Psalm 23 out loud. What words or phrases stick out to you? Why?

Now read John 10:11-13. How does this passage and Psalm 23 relate?

Ask God to encourage you not only for today, but also for tomorrow. Write down any thoughts, tunes, or images that pop into your head.

reflection

Think back to a time where God strengthened you for today and tomorrow. Recognize His faithfulness and thank Him for it.

Jesus, as my Shepherd, You have guided me. You were faithful then, You are faithful now, and You will be faithful in the future. I thank you for walking with me, guiding me, protecting me, and revealing Yourself to me. I thank you for being my Shepherd. Help me to follow You! Amen.

able

> God is able to do far more than we could ever ask for or
> imagine. He does everything by his power that is
> working in us.
> EPHESIANS 3:20 (NIRV)

As a kid, I fondly remember getting many piggy-back rides from my dad. Sometimes it was so I could see over a crowd of people. Other times it was because my legs were giving out from trying to keep stride with the grown-ups. I was okay with needing a little extra help back then. In fact, I welcomed it. But what happens to us as we get older?

Suddenly if we are not able to do something on our own, we feel small, embarrassed, or inadequate. But here's a reality check: we weren't meant to get through life on our own. God gives us others here on earth to help us through our seasons of waiting, but more importantly, He gives us direct access to Him and His Son, Jesus. How cool is that?!

I've tried to do a lot of things on my own. Things that I was clearly not meant to do by myself. Because of my stubbornness, I've tripped and fallen more times than I can count. I still stumble, but no matter how far I fall, I've learned that God is there. He's ready and willing to pick me up so I can rest my weary legs and see that there is something bigger happening around me. I might think something is impossible, like persevering through the next storm, but God has all the power to make it possible. He is able even when I am not. For this, I am incredibly grateful.

Take a moment to read Ephesians 3:20. God is able to do more than what?

God is able to do more than we could ever ask, think, or imagine. More than we can imagine? I love that. God is so much bigger, mightier, and more wonderful than we can even comprehend. I can imagine some pretty awesome things, and to know that I serve a God who can do infinitely more than my wildest, craziest dreams is something I am thankful for.

It's important to realize however, that even though God is able, it doesn't mean He will. God is able to heal here on earth. But with my dad, He chose to heal him once and for all in his eternal home.

God is able to get you that dream job, but there might be something more important He wants to teach you in the meantime.

God is able to introduce you to your future spouse tomorrow, but He may have a plan that's better than anything you could conjure up in your own mind.

God is able to put a stop to the season of waiting we are in, but God also wants us to learn how to persevere. That perseverance leads to strengthened character, which precedes an increased hope in Him.

What does 1 Chronicles 29:11-12 tell us about God?

God is able, and He is also all-knowing, just, and sovereign. Even though we may wish for God to grant us all that we ask, we can also practice thanking Him for His sovereignty. Thanking Him that He always knows what's best for His children. Being grateful that no matter what, He is always looking out for His kids, cheering for them to turn around. To choose the right path. To recognize they cannot do it all on their own. And He is ready to take their hand and lead them when they do.

Write Jesus' words in Matthew 19:26 and underline them, bold them, star them, draw circles around them, shout them out loud...whatever you need to do to make sure this truth begins to sink in.

So what are you dreaming about during this season of waiting? Are you hoping that your kids will grow to love and honor the Lord with all their hearts? Is it for emotional healing of wrongs done against you long ago? Are you dreaming of starting a new business on mere pennies? Is your greatest hope today that your spouse will return to you ready to give the marriage another try? Whatever it is, keep dreaming, imagining, hoping, and thanking. Why? Because what's impossible for us is ALWAYS possible with God. Every. Single. Thing.

dive deeper

Look up the following verses and write out key words or phrases:

Job 42:2

Jeremiah 32:27

Mark 10:27

Does your view of God match the descriptions in these verses? What can you do to remind yourself of who God is?

reflection

What is something that seems impossible to you right now?
Talk to God and ask Him to help you begin to see your times
of wait as opportunities to grow in character and hope.
Write out some things that you can be grateful for during
this season of your life with the knowledge that God is
bigger than anything we're facing.

Dear God, all things are possible with You. You are
sovereign over all of Your creation. Open my heart to what
You want to teach me during my seasons of wait. Help me
to be grateful for the opportunities You have given me to
grow and persevere. Thank you that when I am not able,
You are. Amen.

discovering peace

Not that I am speaking of being in need, for I have learned in whatever situation I am to be content. I know how to be brought low, and I know how to abound. In any and every circumstance, I have learned the secret of facing plenty and hunger, abundance and need.

PHILIPPIANS 4:11-12

When I first came across Philippians 4, immediately my eyes were drawn to verses 6-7, "[D]o not be anxious...the peace of God...will guard your hearts." I wanted that peace and was looking for any way to get it. According to these verses, it seems easy enough, right? It seems the equation is: prayer + thankfulness = peace.

Well, I must admit, math has never been a strength of mine. I did my best to follow these steps—praying and being thankful—however, it didn't result with total peace. Have you felt this way too? Maybe it's because this equation isn't the solution.

So now what? What *is* the solution?

In order to answer this question, we need to figure out why the equation doesn't work in the first place. Let's take a step back. In our haste to find peace *now*, sometimes we tend rush into the "do not be anxious" command, and as a result, we miss the source of where our peace actually comes from.

Take a look back at verse 5. Did you catch that? "The Lord is at hand." Because He is here with us, we do not need to be anxious about anything! This sentence eliminates the need for the equation!

God is our peace! If we pray without realizing His nearness is our peace, our anxious prayers will become anxious thoughts for the enemy to feed on, distracting us from building our relationship with the Prince of Peace. Because God is near, we can pray to Him and cast our anxieties on Him always.

Take a moment to look up 1 Peter 5:6-10. What stands out to you about overcoming anxiety and standing firm in your faith in these verses?

Finding peace is no longer about how we pray, what we do, or what action steps we try to follow. It first starts with realizing and believing in our hearts, that He is at hand!

Often times, peace doesn't come in the form of an immediately answered prayer. It's simply knowing that He is near, that He hasn't abandoned us, and that He will walk with us through all seasons of our lives.

Think back to a time when you were in a season of the unknown, maybe feeling scared. Did you want someone to hold your hand? Someone to comfort you and be with you until the scene became familiar?

If you answered, "Yes," I'm right there with you. As a young child, I remember scooping up my cat when I needed to go down into our creepy basement. It wasn't that I thought the cat would protect me. I knew he would run away the second I put him down, but his presence calmed me. If we can find comfort like this in the presence of another human (or animal), how much more comfort do you think we can find in the presence of Jesus, the Prince of Peace?

As we move forward today, let's not get stuck on trying to solve this impossible equation forgetting that our true peace comes when we choose to draw near to God. Remember, He has promised to never leave or forsake us, and we are His daughters in Christ. Next time overwhelming feelings threaten to steal your joy, take a step back and remind yourself that the Lord is always near.

dive deeper

Read Philippians 4:4-7 again. How can you respond to the command, "[D]o not be anxious about anything," even during seasons of wait and hardship?

How is God's peace described in the following verses?

Isaiah 26:3

John 14:27

John 16:33

2 Thessalonians 3:16

reflection

Talk to God about your relationship with Him. What do you tend to worry about most? Have you experienced His peace when you needed it before?

Jesus, please help me today as I seek Your peace. No matter what journey I have to travel, I want to be reminded You are always near. When I forget this and feel overwhelmed by anxieties, help me to remember Your promises. I choose to walk with You, always. Amen.

gratitude for empathy

Rejoice with those who rejoice, weep with those who weep.
ROMANS 12:15

I'll never forget a frank conversation I had with God a few years ago. There I sat, on a hot summer day, casually letting Him know this plan for my life wasn't the one I wanted. It was a pretty simple conversation that went something like this:

God, I don't like this. Please take away this story of mine. I don't want to wait anymore. I don't want to live with this longing. I don't want to feel like I am fighting. I'm tired of feeling imprisoned in this season.

Then of course, because He is God and I put myself in a place to listen, He changed my perspective and redirected my thinking. Later that day, I was listening to a sermon by Pastor Craig Groeschel, and he said a thought-provoking statement, one that instantly changed my thinking: "My prison can become His pulpit."

Wham.

I don't know what you're going through this season. It may be infertility. It may be dealing with the loss of your spouse. Maybe it's the daily stresses of parenting, a weight struggle, an addiction, an unstable parent, or the pain of watching a friend hurt themselves.

This is your chance to let God use your story to glorify Him. Even more so, your season, whatever it is, as hard or easy or happy or sad, is the opportunity God has given you to relate to others exactly like you. God has given you, yes YOU, the one reading this today, an opportunity unlike anyone else. He has made your heart sensitive enough to empathize to someone else in a similar waiting-world.

I am grateful for the broad heart of empathy that God gives all of us. But as I continue to live out my wait, I am even more thankful that He has made my heart uniquely tender to those struggling with infertility and pregnancy loss. I can listen, mourn, celebrate, and reflect with those who know these emotions.

The same goes for you! You understand what it's like to be a single mom in a way that I don't. Or a widow. Or a recent grad trying to launch a career.

Becoming a person who *really* knows how someone else is feeling requires a costly education. We have to walk through it ourselves first. In order to relate and say, "Me too," we have to march up the painful hill first. But it's in that uphill walk where God provides us training unlike anything else. Simply put, God prepares us to become an answer to someone else's prayer in their own time of need.

Can you pause today and give thanks to God for the education and training you've had the privilege to receive? Write out your prayer below.

We have this *beautiful* opportunity to take this struggle of ours and use it as a way to relate to others. Our stories give us the unique ability to offer comfort that isn't generic. At some point, God is going to use this season of our lives to bring Him so much glory and soothe someone in need. Isn't that a humbling feeling? When I think about this painful season as an opportunity to display His love and goodness despite the pain, I can't help but feel honored. Honored that He would allow me to be part of it. Honored that He would use someone like me.

I understand how completely insane that sounds. But what if we receive this season as a gift? Something that Christ is educating us in so that we can be more like Him, so that we can bring God glory by being the hands and feet of Jesus. That's something to be eternally grateful for.

We are learning things, Friend. We have such a unique chance to grow as a result of our experiences. To tenderly love others in our seasons because we understand. So now, instead of asking, "Why," we can ask, "Now what?"

dive deeper

Take a moment to look up 2 Corinthians 1:2-4. Write out what this means to you in your own words.

Your struggles can become your ministry! Pause and reflect on what God might want to do in your life. What do you feel like He is saying to you?

reflection

How have you seen Christ work in your heart as a result of being in this season? If you could encourage someone going through the same thing today, what would you say to them?

Take another step. Brainstorm ideas on how God could use your story. Maybe it's not today or next week, but next year or ten years from now. How would you like to see Him use you?

Do you know anyone today who could use a little extra encouragement? Drop them a note in the mail or send them an email. When we remember that we have the chance to be used, it changes our attitudes; it changes our hearts. It cultivates a soul of gratitude.

Lord, thank you. Thank you for allowing me this unique opportunity to show compassion to others just as You have shown me. I ask now for eyes that see those in need and for You to transform my heart, allowing me to see the ministry opportunity ahead. Continue to help me see trials as joy and to love Your people. Amen *grateful for eternity*

He will wipe every tear from their eyes. There will be no more death or mourning or crying or pain, for the old order of things has passed away.
REVELATION 21:4

My MRI results have come back: Normal. The voicemail from my neurologist: No need to schedule another appointment. Direction from my primary doctor: Your Vitamin D levels are low, so take 5000 IUs a day and you'll notice things begin to climb back to normal.

WHAT?! One day, I'm being diagnosed with MS; the neurologist shaking his head at anything other and preparing me for the worst. Then the next, a simple vitamin deficiency?

Why jump to worst-case and *then* backtrack? Talk about stressful.

But here's the deal. This is what I'm learning in the wait of it all. When we put our faith in Christ, we are saved for all eternity. Nothing can touch our souls and our promise of a better tomorrow, because Jesus Himself promises to fulfill these things.

But the interim time? The days and years we are waiting on this earth before we enter the kingdom of God? We're sure to experience some curveballs. There'll be some disasters that strike at high noon, diseases that prowl through the darkness, and arrows that fly in the day; a job loss, miscarriage, or a disheartening health diagnosis.

Why? Because we live in a fallen world, and this time is *all* the enemy has. Satan has only been given this short timeline here on earth to do everything in his weak power to lead us away from Christ. He knows what will scare us and deter us from the life God wants us to live, so he'll spit on our trial, throw obstacles in our face, and play mind games with our vulnerable selves—all for that purpose, and again, for only this time. Because the second we step into our Heaven, he can't touch us.

Seems intense, right? I grew up in a conservative denomination with barely a mention of the Holy Spirit until I got to college. No one wanted to talk about evil or spiritual attacks. And frankly, to this day, I still don't want to! It seems easier, more peaceful, more comfortable without. I prefer ignorance; it often is bliss.

But when life attacks and seasons of waiting are just downright annoying, ignorance is not bliss. We will face trials here on earth, Jesus promised that in John 16:33. And when the bad news comes, the human way is to be paralyzed by fear and stuck in disillusionment.

Like my situation? If I would have just known my dizziness and weird tingling were due to a vitamin deficiency, I wouldn't have wasted another second of worry! I would have just popped the vitamins, downed some water, and brushed that fear off my shoulder.

The enemy though loved nothing more than prolonging the situation, darkening the days a bit more with the unknown, and tempting me to doubt my victory and my hope. All the mental exhaustion, the hours I spent crying, and the moments I lived in defeat? Exactly what he wanted for me. *Not* what God wanted for me.

But when we know the truth, it's a different story. It sets us free, because we hold the ultimate victory. We don't have to waste our time in the darkness of the unknown or the scary what-if's of the future, because through Christ's death and resurrection, our future *is* secure, and our eternity *is* in His hands. We can stand strong, knowing we will receive the crown of life and bask in a perfect relationship with God forevermore—with *no* more tears, *no* more heartache, *no* more waiting—if we just keep the faith.

Whatever waiting you're in, it's a guarantee that the enemy will want to play around with your situation. His attacks are always the same: you'll be tempted to doubt God's goodness and His plan. You'll feel a sense of hopelessness wash in and probably cry a few tears of sorrow. You may wonder how things will ever be different, if the Promised Land will ever come, and how God could ever save you. Nothing novel, but even still, it seems to get us every time.

But today, let's refuse to let the defeat creep in. Let's instead focus our eyes on our eternal home, the room Jesus is preparing for us in His Father's house. And let's find gratefulness in knowing that no matter what attacks we face today, we are promised a future of ultimate victory in Heaven. And nothing can snatch that away from us!

So don't let this world trip you up, Friend. Stay strong. Keep your chin up. Trust in God. Share your testimony. And remember, *victory is yours.*

dive deeper

What do these verses tell us about our eternity?

Isaiah 25:6-9

John 14:1-6

Revelation 7:13-17

Revelation 22:3-7

Jesus has gone to prepare a room for us in Heaven, our future home. Read John 16:5-15. While we wait, what has Jesus sent us in place of His human presence? He said it was best for Him to go, so the Advocate could come. How are you inviting the Holy Spirit into your everyday life?

reflection

Share about a time when the enemy threw obstacles in your path. Was it easy to deflect and move forward in faith? Or how did you allow fear to creep in?

How can you be grateful for the promise of eternity today?

Jesus, I praise You that You are Lord over all things. You are sovereign over the timetable of this world, yet even still, You see me through every detail of my life. Thank you for promising me a future home with You and an eternity that is secured. I'm so grateful for this ultimate truth. In Your powerful name, I pray. Amen.

gratitude in the wait

"And I can always give thanks because an all powerful God always has all these things - all things - under control."
ANN VOSKAMP, *One Thousand Gifts*

No matter what life throws our way, we can always give thanks because we serve a God who is all-powerful, all-knowing, wholly just, and full of love. In Him, we can find peace, contentment, and true life through the power of gratitude and His grace.

What was your biggest takeaway from this week?

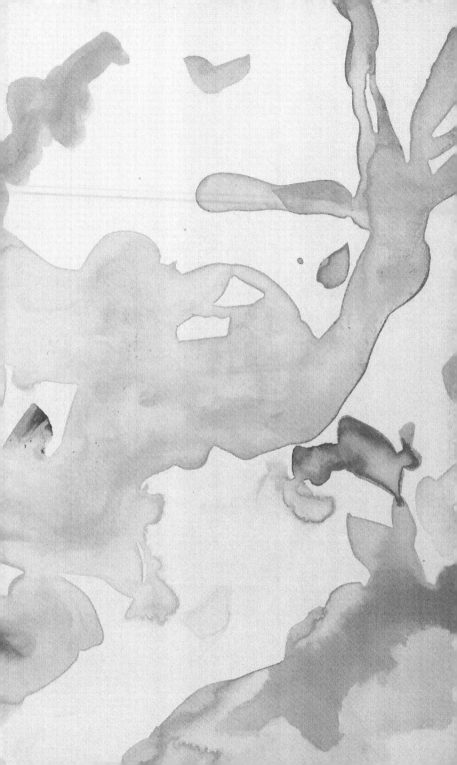

a final thought from the authors

Dear Friend,

We're all hoping for something. Being in the wait is not limited to only a select few. Therefore, each one of us must learn to wait, knowing God is on our side.

This study didn't cover everything. We do hope, however, these words have helped you feel more equipped to make the most of every season—no matter what each one entails.

We pray you can use our words, and more importantly, God's truth, to help you face into today and the days to come. Friend, continue to see seasons of waiting as opportunities to grow in your relationship with Christ and bring glory to our Creator. Waiting provides us an opportunity to actively listen, persevere, find community, experience joy, claim victory, and live gratefully.

Thank you for joining us on this journey as we learned more about what it means to live fully in the wait. We sincerely hope that God spoke to your heart in this study and that you can carry these principles beyond the pages of this book. God bless!

Much love,
Heidi, Courtney, Holly, Amanda, and Chelsea

about the authors

COURTNEY FRASIER
Week 1 Author
IG: @acupofco
acupofco.com

Courtney is a pun-loving creative who lives in Minnesota with her husband, Dave. Courtney finds great joy in seeing the small details of life connect to the big plan God has for His children. Encouraging others, in a big or small way, makes her soul sing! Among her favorite things are family time and cooking.

AMANDA JASS
Week 2 Author

Amanda is a wife, mama, and a born-and-raised Minnesota gal. She and her husband have two daughters who are beautiful answers to lots of prayer. Family walks, a good DIY project, and sipping coffee with friends are a few of her favorite activities. She has a background working in higher education and children's ministry, and she enjoys her new primary role of working in her home.

HOLLY HOLT
Week 3 Author
IG: @hollyjoyholt
hollyholtdesign.com

Holly is a lover of life who thrives on hugs and a good conversation. She designs products with purpose for Holly Holt Design, and helps women live fully—no matter what season they are in. When she isn't working, Holly enjoys reading a good book and spending time outdoors with her husband, Derek, and daughter, Eliana.

CHELSEA RITCHIE
Week 4 Author
IG: @chels819
trialsbringjoy.com

Chelsea is a Midwestern girl who loves connecting with others about infertility, motherhood, and living authentically. She's been married to Josh for double-digit years. Their twins, Kirsten and Logan, were joyfully welcomed to their family after nearly a decade of waiting and loss. Chelsea loves a good cup of coffee, a cozy bookshop, and mindless reality TV. Her heart finds joy in untangling the trials in life and allowing God to help her find beauty every day.

HEIDI ANDERSON
Week 5 Author
IG: @thismotherhen

Heidi is a writer, speaker, wife, and stay-at-home mom, who crafts daily devotionals for Eagle Brook Church, cleans up cheerio spills around the clock, and drinks coffee like a Gilmore. Ultimately, Heidi's passion and the fuel behind her writing is that Christ followers would realize, know, and claim the victory God offers His people—in the mundane, amidst the heartache, and on top of the highest mountains.

special thanks

Cover Watercolor Art: Courtney Frasier
Cover Lettering: Heidi Anderson

additional resources

Books

Crash the Chatterbox by Steven Furtick

Sun Stands Still by Steven Furtick

Everything Bitter is Sweet by Sara Hagerty

A Praying Life by Paul E. Miller

Bittersweet by Shauna Niequist

Finding Faith in the Dark by Laurie Short

Mended by Angie Smith

Websites/Blogs

Life Lived Beautifully

Proverbs 31

She Reads Truth

citations

"Confident." *Merriam Webster.com*. Merriam-Webster, 2015. Web. 8 June 2015.

Furtick, Steven. *Crash the Chatterbox*. Colorado Springs, CO: Multnomah Books, 2014. Print.

Gladden, Steve. "Biblical Community on Mission." *Saddleback Church*. Web.

Groeschel, Craig. "Why." *Life Church*. Web.

Hatmaker, Jen. *7 : An Experimental Mutiny against Excess*. Nashville, Tenn.: B&H Pub. Group, 2012.

Niequist, Shauna. *Bread & Wine : A Love Letter to Life Around the Table, With Recipes*. Grand Rapids, Mich.: Zondervan, 2013.

Niequist, Shauna. *Cold Tangerines: Celebrating the Extraordinary Nature of Everyday Life*. Grand Rapids, Mich. Zondervan, 2007. Print.

"Patient." *Merriam Webster.com*. Merriam-Webster, 2015. Web. 13 June 2015.

Strand, Jason. "More Than Happy: Joy in the Struggle." Eagle Brook Church, Lino Lakes, Minn. 15 June 2015. Audio.

Voskamp, Ann. *One Thousand Gifts: A Dare to Live Fully Right Where You Are*. Grand Rapids, Mich.: Zondervan, 2010. Print.

"Wait." *Merriam Webster.com*. Merriam-Webster, 2015. Web. 7 June 2015.

Made in the USA
Middletown, DE
15 November 2018